ROCHESTER

An Urban Biography

VIRGINIA M. WRIGHT-PETERSON

MINNESOTA HISTORICAL SOCIETY PRESS

CLEAN
WATER
LAND &
LEGACY
AMENDMENT

Cities, like people, are always changing, and the history of that change
is the city's biography. The Urban Biography Series illuminates the unique character
of each city, weaving in the hidden stories of place, politics, and identity that
continue to shape its residents' lives.

Photos from the History Center of Olmsted County are credited to HCOC;
those from the W. Bruce Fye Center for the History of Medicine (Mayo Clinic Archive),
Rochester, are credited to WBFCHM. The images from the *Rochester Post Bulletin* are
reprinted with permission, which we gratefully acknowledge.

mnhspress.org

The Minnesota Historical Society Press is a member of the
Association of University Presses.

Manufactured in the United States of America

10 9 8 7 6 5 4 3 2 1

♾ The paper used in this publication meets the minimum requirements
of the American National Standard for Information Sciences—Permanence for
Printed Library Materials, ANSI Z39.48–1984.

International Standard Book Number
ISBN: 978-1-68134-228-3 (paper)
ISBN: 978-1-68134-229-0 (e-book)

Library of Congress Control Number: 2022933906

This and other Minnesota Historical Society Press books are
available from popular e-book vendors.

Contents

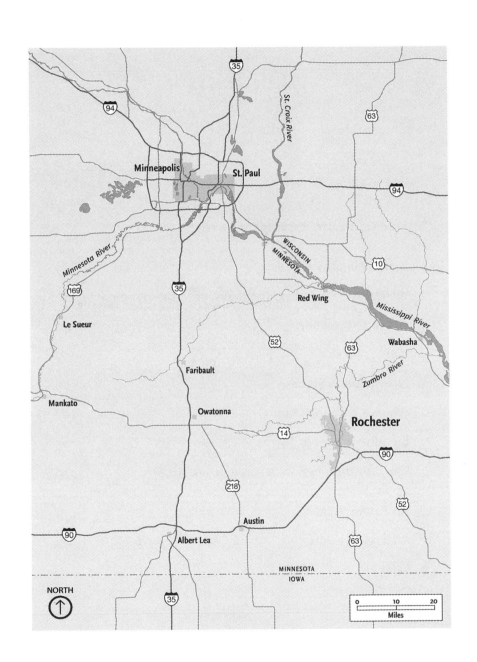

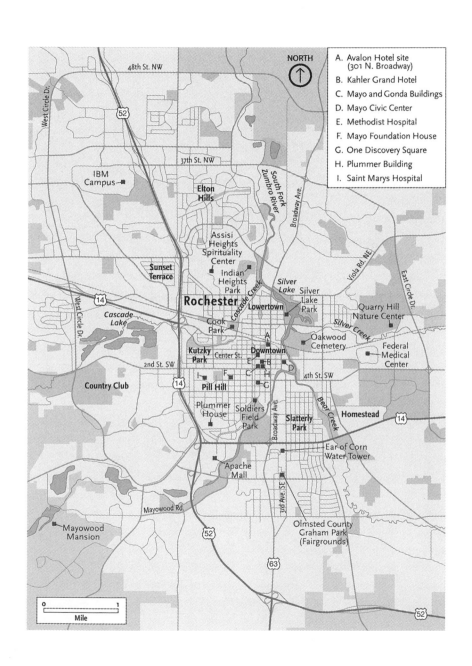

NORTH
↑

A. Avalon Hotel site (301 N. Broadway)
B. Kahler Grand Hotel
C. Mayo and Gonda Buildings
D. Mayo Civic Center
E. Methodist Hospital
F. Mayo Foundation House
G. One Discovery Square
H. Plummer Building
I. Saint Marys Hospital

48th St. NW

West Circle Dr.

52

37th St. NW

IBM Campus

Elton Hills

South Fork Zumbro River

Broadway Ave.

Assisi Heights Spirituality Center

Sunset Terrace

Indian Heights Park

Viola Rd. NE

East Circle Dr.

Rochester

Silver Lake

Silver Lake Park

Cascade Creek

Lowertown

Quarry Hill Nature Center

West Circle Dr.

14

Cascade Lake

Cook Park

Silver Creek

Oakwood Cemetery

Federal Medical Center

Kutzky Park

Center St.

Downtown

2nd St. SW

A

E   B

14

I   F   C   H

4th St. SW

Country Club

Pill Hill

G

D

Plummer House

Soldiers Field Park

Broadway Ave.

Slatterly Park

Bear Creek

Homestead

14

Ear of Corn Water Tower

Apache Mall

3rd Ave. SE

Mayowood Rd.

52

Mayowood Mansion

Olmsted County Graham Park (Fairgrounds)

63

0   1
Mile

52

Knowing a Place,
Knowing Ourselves

It is possible to live in a city most of your life and think you know that place well, but actually not really know it. I have resided in Rochester, Minnesota, since I took my first breath at Saint Marys Hospital in 1959. I have also lived in Minneapolis and Duluth; Scottsdale, Arizona; Lincoln, Nebraska; Algiers, Algeria; and Contingency Operating Base (COB) Speicher in Iraq—but I have lived the majority of my sixty-two years in Rochester, where my grandchildren represent the seventh generation of our family to live in southeastern Minnesota. I thought I knew the story of Rochester intimately until I began poring through documents at the local history center and talking with people with lived experiences quite different from mine. I soon learned there were missing pieces and absolute voids in the story I knew, and I am certain there are many more pieces yet to be revealed.

The history of the city of Rochester has been masked by the story of the rise of Mayo Clinic. As grand and impressive as that story is, it is not the entire story of this city. Much of the narrative has been left behind, left out. I am focusing on several threads of the story that are not well known to me and to most of the city's residents, and although not all of them are complimentary, they create a richer, more complex history that we can celebrate, grieve, and learn. These stories explain, in part, why Rochester remained so homogenous until very recently. Embarking on a more complete history will help forge a stronger, more resilient community, building on the city's heritage of innovation and collaboration.

Although my approach in this book is generally chronological, beginning with the Native American presence and ending with today's Destination Medical Center growth initiative, I deviate occasionally in order to more fully address some topics when it seems more readable to do so. For example, in the second chapter I trace modes of transportation beginning with rivers and stagecoach routes and continuing through the end of the passenger train access in 1963, allowing readers to get a sense of the development and impact of transportation rather than inserting bits about the topic throughout the book. The next chapter loops back to the cyclone of 1883 and covers the origination of Saint Marys Hospital and the Mayo medical practice through 1914. It is my hope that this tactic will give readers a sense of important themes within the context of Rochester's overall history.

While I was growing up in Rochester in the 1960s and 1970s, I believed there were few Native Americans in the area because they had not actually lived here. I thought they only occasionally passed through when hunting. As I researched this book, I learned that Indigenous people spent more time here than I realized. I also learned that men from Rochester formed a militia to resist the "depredations of the Indians" in the US–Dakota War of 1862, and a Rochester artist achieved national renown by graphically exploiting the conflict.

I also believed that people of color just chose to live in more urban areas rather than in Rochester, and their choice resulted in our town being homogenously white. I learned that the Ku Klux Klan was active in Rochester in the 1920s, few hotels allowed people of color to rent rooms, and in the early years Mayo Clinic required Jews, Blacks, and Greeks to put down a deposit before they could receive care. Further, Mayo Clinic administrators placed racially discriminatory covenants on property they sold. I was startled to see one of these covenants on the deed of the first home my husband and I bought in 1983 near Saint Marys Hospital.

By the 1950s, Rochester's homogeneity was a significant factor in the selection criteria as IBM's leaders sought a site for a large plant. Hecklers harassed residents participating in a civil rights march through downtown Rochester in 1963, and that evening a burning cross appeared in front of a hotel that catered to people of color. The Rochester newspaper editorialized against future civil rights marches.

I also learned that a large section of the cemetery where the Mayo families and other influential people are buried includes hundreds, possibly a thousand, unmarked graves. My husband, father, grandparents, and great-grandparents are buried in this cemetery, too.

Knowing these truths has changed me. I can see my family and my identity revealed and impacted at nearly every turn of this evolving story. So often what is not told, what is absent in a story, reveals as much as what is known.

I researched and wrote the biography of Rochester in the context of extraordinary, disruptive events swirling around our state and nation. The first case of COVID-19 was reported in Rochester on March 11, 2020. Two days later, Governor Tim Walz issued the first of many peacetime emergency orders, closing public schools, then closing restaurants and bars; on March 25, he signed an order to shelter in place. Only essential workers—health-care providers, law enforcement, and others needed to operate for critical infrastructure—were allowed to work outside their homes. We ran to grocery stores to stock up, many of us thinking two weeks of food would be sufficient to weather this emergency. Toilet paper flew off the shelves. Schoolchildren found themselves suddenly at home, peering at their teachers through tablet and laptop screens. Teachers, with almost no notice, created lesson plans that could be delivered virtually.

My job allowed me to work from home. I began writing under lockdown and through months of daily reports of cases, hospitalizations, and deaths. As this book goes to press in March 2022, more than 40,000 people have been infected with COVID and 170 people have died from COVID in Olmsted County—where Rochester is located. In Minnesota, nearly 12,000 people have died, and of the 80 million cases of COVID in the United States, one million people have died. The deaths worldwide are approaching six million, and the Omicron variant is taking hold internationally when we thought the pandemic was transitioning into a less lethal endemic.

In addition to facing the consequences of COVID, we have lived in varying degrees of fear, isolation, depression, and anger over the last two years. The causes and manifestations are many: bitter disputes over masking and vaccinations; the murder of George Floyd on May 25, 2020, in Minneapolis, igniting demonstrations throughout the world calling for an end to racism; a sharply divided political arena, as followers of a former president continue to question the outcome of the 2020 election and voting rights are hotly contested; a summer of drought and wildfires that brought a smoky haze to Rochester and the region, causing health alerts. Many days while I was writing, the sun and moon rose and set amid red- and orange-painted skies, reflecting the smoke and an apocalyptic aura.

Documenting a fuller version of Rochester's past in this context, one of the most disruptive times of recorded history in Minnesota and the United States, creates a unique vantage point: we can see ourselves in a new light. Although we have read about world wars, past pandemics, massive wildfires, hurricanes, and civil unrest, most of us have not lived through a period this deeply disruptive. What we are experiencing will be long remembered and analyzed. The actions that individuals and communities take, or do not take, make them who they are. A disruptive time like this breaks open the status quo and creates the opportunity for transformative change. Rochester's history is full of people who made bold moves and people who chose to stand on the sidelines.

Because my perspective is both heavily influenced and limited by my experiences living in Rochester as a cisgender, straight, middle-class white woman, I have incorporated some of my story into this narrative as sidebars. This allows me to remind myself and my readers of my limitations. My research has convinced me more than ever that my identity and my perspective is inextricably linked to Rochester, Minnesota. There is no way that I could create an "objective" biography of this place, so I am sharing what I learned with transparency about my place in this story when it is relevant.

I am hopeful that readers will understand the story of Rochester more completely and be inspired to look deeper into the stories of their own places, illuminating lost and suppressed narratives. A better future is possible if we move forward in the context of a more inclusive history. For Rochester, reckoning with the past—even aspects of it that are regrettable—as well as celebrating the well-known achievements will serve the community well as it builds on a heritage of innovation and collaboration.

CHAPTER 1

Indian Heights

A tree-covered bluff in northeast Rochester rises above a neighborhood, two strip malls, the Zumbro River, and a dam forming Silver Lake. Beginning in 1896, developers used limestone quarried from the bluff to construct buildings in the growing city. After the quarry closed, the woods were frequented by wildlife and picnickers. In 1974, residents in the neighborhood convinced the city to purchase thirty-seven acres for a park, protecting the natural area from development.

Indian Heights Park, 2021. *Photo by Brendan Bush*

Although the park was named Indian Heights, few people in Rochester thought seriously about the presence of Dakota people on the bluff and the surrounding area until 2010, when a local group of mountain bikers proposed creating a trail through the park, sparking an intense debate among residents living nearby, the bikers, and Dakota people. The mountain bike enthusiasts wanted a place for riding steep hills and trails. Neighbors argued that mountain biking would destroy the natural environment of the park and disturb people wishing to go for a quiet hike or picnic. Many neighbors also wanted to respect the sacredness of burial grounds believed to exist on the bluff. Several Dakota people came forward and recounted the importance of the land to their ancestors, bringing a renewed awareness of the Dakota community to Rochester after it had been latent for over a century.

The importance of the area later known as Rochester to Dakota people begins much earlier. One Dakota creation story holds that people originated from the stars of the Milky Way at Bdote Mni Sota, the intersection of waterways now commonly called the Mississippi and Minnesota Rivers. Dakota lived in summer villages along these two great rivers and their many tributaries, and they moved throughout the region during the year, hunting game and gathering foods in season. They named one of the Mississippi's tributaries Wazi Ozu Wakpa, meaning "river where the pines grow"; the French referred to it as Rivière des Embarras ("river of obstructions"), and today it is known as the Zumbro River, which runs through Rochester.

Dakota oral traditions and European written histories describe the initially symbiotic relationships among the Dakota and European explorers

Growing up in Rochester in the 1960s and '70s, I was unaware of any Native American presence. My grandfather kept a few stone arrowheads he found in nearby fields in old pill bottles stuffed with cotton. My Girl Scout troop visited with Chief Winneshiek of the Ho-Chunk nation, referred to as Winnebago at the time. Otherwise, I do not recall mention of Native Americans or Indian Heights.

and fur traders in southeastern Minnesota beginning in the 1680s: Europeans provided metal tools, cloth, and guns that Dakota families wanted
in exchange for pelts. Pierre-Charles Le Sueur, a Frenchman and one of
the first Europeans to enter the region, noted the presence of the Dakota
along the upper branch of Wazi Ozu Wakpa. His observations were
drawn on a map of the region in 1697. Despite the presence of Indigenous people, the French claimed most of Minnesota west of the Mississippi, including the area now known as Rochester, during the 1700s, as
part of the Louisiana Territory.

The US government initiated treaties with Native American nations
on the East Coast, pushing them west and resulting in overlapping ter-
ritories and conflicts. In 1803, during the presidency of Thomas Jef-
ferson, the United States paid France $15 million—approximately $18
per square mile, or four cents an acre—for the Louisiana Territory. Two
years later, federal officials began negotiating treaties intended to remove
Native Americans from land in the Midwest, accelerating the westward
movement of European Americans.

As speculators, followed by settlers, pushed across the continent, sur-
veyors spread out like ants, marking off the prairies and forests into
squares of land with stakes and string. In the eyes of the US government, the country was a grid of square miles divided into blocks of 640
acres, called sections. Thirty-six sections made up a township. Townships
were grouped into counties and counties into states. European American
settlers wanted to own the land, build fences, and plow under prairies
to make farm fields, replicating a form of land use and ownership from
their homelands, a practice that intrinsically conflicted with the Dakota
people's relationship with the land. They call the earth Ina, mother. No
one owns Ina.

Under tremendous pressure, the Bdewakaŋtuŋwaŋ, Waȟpekute,
Sisitoŋwaŋ, and Waȟpetoŋwaŋ bands of Dakota ceded the land that
became Rochester through the Treaties of Traverse des Sioux and Men-
dota of 1851. Through these agreements, the Dakota gave up 24 million
acres in Minnesota Territory for the equivalent of 7.5 cents per acre, to
be paid in annuities over fifty years. A significant portion of the pay-
ment immediately went to retire debts claimed by fur companies that

had been trading with the Dakota until the price for fur fell due to a saturated market. The Dakota ceded all of southern Minnesota—about 43 percent of the state's area—retaining a strip of land seventy miles long and twenty miles wide along the Minnesota River. When this treaty was signed, the US government owed the Dakota significant amounts unpaid from previous agreements. They were buying on credit.

Indian Heights was part of the land transferred as a part of the treaties in 1851. The area along the south branch of the Zumbro River was claimed and renamed by newcomers. George and Henrietta Head arrived in July 1854 and built their home near the river. The following year, the Minnesota territorial government designated Olmsted County, naming it for David Olmsted, the first mayor of St. Paul. In 1858, Rochester was legally incorporated and became the county seat.

The town's new residents noted the presence of the Dakota as they moved into the area. According to Joseph Leonard's 1883 history of Olmsted County, "For one or two years after the first settlement of the county there were small bands of Sioux Indians roving about, hunting in the woods and fishing in the streams. . . . They never molested anyone, but being hungry, they demanded the means to satisfy the cravings of their appetites." Leonard, like many of the new residents, saw the seasonal appearance as "roving" and did not understand Dakota cultural requirements for sharing and generosity.

According to Leonard, one of the last Dakota encampments along the southern branch of Wazi Ozu Wakpa below the Indian Heights bluff in Rochester occurred in the fall of 1854. Two hundred Dakota stayed in the bend of the river. During their six-week stay, three Dakota men and one woman died, possibly of smallpox, and they were buried on "a bluff nearly west of the site where Cascade Mill" was later built. They moved their encampment a short distance to the south, and four more Dakota died, including a leader. They hired two white men to assist with the burial, which took place on the bluff because of its sacred location: the highest point of elevation in the area with an eastern slope facing the rising run. Soon after the burial, they moved their encampment again, leaving a young woman named Winona behind because she was ill. After a few days, she recovered and walked to the nearby home of Mr. and Mrs. James Bucklin, who took her in until they could inform the "unfeeling savages" of her whereabouts. A leader and their healer came to get her. They gave the Bucklins a knife case and moccasins in gratitude.

Leonard notes that by the following spring, in 1855, "the Indians all left, and this was the last which was seen of the Sioux in the county." This statement announces the departure of the Dakota as if they had simply chosen to move, rather than being forced to do so by the treaties signed in 1851.

Members of another nation, the Ho-Chunk (or Winnebago), had also lived in the Rochester area. Their traditional territory was east of the Mississippi River, in what is now known as Wisconsin. But by the mid-1850s, whites who wanted their lands for agriculture and lumber had forced the Ho-Chunk to move three times: from Wisconsin to Iowa in the 1830s, to Long Prairie in central Minnesota in 1848, and to a reservation about sixty miles west of Rochester on the Le Sueur River in 1855. Leonard's history of Olmsted County mentions that "small parties . . . were occasionally seen strolling back and forth through the county on their way to and from their former home in Wisconsin. The Winnebagoes were very fond of gambling, and for stakes would put up their buffalo robes or other articles which they might have about them. It is said that a small party of these Indians camped a short time on or near Zumbro street, a few rods from the court house, in the year 1862."

One of Rochester's earliest settlers recalled the presence of the Ho-Chunk people in the region. Marion Louisa Sloan, who proudly traced her ancestry to the governor of Plymouth Colony and to a mate on the *Mayflower*, came to Rochester as a child with her family in April 1856, just two years after the town was established. Marion recalled that as they were preparing to leave their home in Massachusetts, her grandmother cried that her daughter was "going to Minnesota to be scalped by the Indians," reflecting a prejudice that inevitably followed some settlers as they relocated in the western states.

After initially living in a log house in Rochester, the Sloans built a board house northwest of the business district. One day, when the children were home with their mother, "the room was suddenly filled with indians. They asked for food and she was too frightened to refuse them. She told them they could have some potatoes, which were in the cellar. A trap door led to the cellar and so frightened was she that she said when she stooped to raise the door she felt her hair rise. The old chief seeing her fright said, 'Me good Indian. Me Winnebago.' Later, several Indians came and slept outdoors near the house. The night was cold and Father and Mother feeling sorry for them loaned them a quilt. . . . We expected the quilt to be returned but in the morning the chief strutted away with it around him." Clearly, the newcomers did not comprehend cultural understandings of gift giving. After recalling the incident about the Ho-Chunk, Sloan transitions to a reminiscence about snakes.

By 1856, according to the *History of Olmsted County,* "most of the red men stole away and very few of them were ever afterward seen in the county." This history makes it sound as if the Dakota had snuck away, or at best that they just moved on by choice, as if leaving was their pref- erence. However, it is clear by 1862 they were no longer welcome. They were exiled.

The painful circumstances and actions that led up to the US–Dakota War are difficult to summarize. Basically, the US government and the settlers who flooded onto the lands of southern Minnesota pushed the Dakota into a confining system that prohibited them from feeding and caring for their families. And then the government forced their leaders to sign away half of their reservation in 1858. The Office of Indian Affairs delayed delivery of the annuity payments that were supposed to help sus- tain the Dakota people, and it did not adequately fulfill its commitments under the treaty to build schools, provide teachers, and supply farming equipment. There were many instances of corruption within the Indian Office, including the theft of annuities and the failure to investigate both the illegal sales of liquor and the abuse of Dakota women by white men.

An infestation of cutworms seriously diminished the harvest of 1861, and a harsh winter followed. In the spring of 1862, the goods and money due to the Dakota from the Indian Office were delayed; the treasury was funding the Civil War, which had begun April 12, 1861. White merchants limited the amount of credit they would grant, indifferent to the serious plight of the Dakota people. The Dakota were starving.

The war began when Dakota men attacked the Redwood Agency on August 18, igniting the bloodshed. In the next few days, they attacked farms, small towns, the city of New Ulm, and Fort Ridgely. About six hundred white settlers and soldiers plus an unknown number of Dakota were killed in the course of the war; descriptions of brutal attacks spread terror among the whites throughout the state. Governor Alexander Ramsey dispatched regiments of the state militia to suppress the "uprising."

Communities responded, including units from Rochester, about one hundred miles east of the conflict in New Ulm. On August 27, the *Rochester Republican* newspaper announced that citizens of Rochester, responding to an executive order proclaimed by Governor Ramsey, met to organize a militia "for the purpose of resisting the depredations of the Indians on our western front." In addition to recruiting volunteers, the citizens procured horses, arms, and ammunition. At the same meeting, they discussed the potential danger from Ho-Chunk living in the area. Deciding there was no immediate threat nearby, they determined there was a greater need for their services on the frontier. Not everyone in town supported the effort; some questioned the governor's authority to organize a military unit, and a few doubted the severity of the danger. The unit proceeded to Fort Snelling to be officially mustered as Company I of the First Regiment of Mounted Rangers, known locally as the Rochester Rangers.

Within weeks, Absalom N. Enoch, a local saloonkeeper in Rochester, also recruited men to form what became Company F of the Ninth Regiment of the Minnesota Infantry, called the Olmsted County Tigers. This unit of a hundred men was commissioned at Fort Snelling on September 24, 1862.

The men from Rochester were committed to keeping the frontier safe and answering President Abraham Lincoln's call for troops to fight in the Civil War on behalf of the Union Army. They were enrolled in multiple companies of Minnesota's Second, Third, and Sixth Regiments, and some of the Rochester men became members of several companies of the Minnesota First Battalion and Third Battery. Some of them spent time on the frontier; many posted at Fort Ridgely, twenty-four miles northeast of New Ulm; and other units went to the South immediately.

Occasionally men in the military units who were fighting the Dakota sent updates to the Rochester newspapers. One man described his unit's march from Fort Snelling and then to Fort Ripley, north of St. Cloud, where they were guarding against unrest among the Ojibwe. As they marched, "teams along the road were pressed into service to convey" the troops. "Cheer after cheer went up as we passed through the little towns, and waving handkerchiefs, and tearful eyes of women greeted us on every bend." They also encountered families leaving as refugees to safer parts of the state. The writer noted that the crops had been abandoned, left standing in the fields: "the country looked as desolate as one could well imagine." This observer provided one of the few relatively balanced accounts printed in a Rochester paper: "The difficulty with the [Ojibwe] arose from an attempt on the part of the Indian agent, Maj. Walker, to swindle them out of their annuities—Walker was obligated to leave, and since his departure no hostile demonstrations have been made."

The status of all Native Americans living in Minnesota, regardless of their involvement in the violence, was debated. Governor Ramsey, addressing the state legislature on September 9, declared, "The Sioux Indians of Minnesota must be exterminated or driven forever beyond the borders of the state," and newspapers repeated the call.

On October 8, 1862, as the imprisoned Dakota men awaited trial, animosity toward Indians grew. The *Rochester Republican* reprinted a scathing profile of Native Americans first published in the paper in nearby La Crosse, Wisconsin: "The Indian is by nature a drunkard or a savage, and always a coward. If he ever ceases to manifest his natural depravity it is because he loves whiskey better than he loves blood. If they sometimes cease butchering each other, or the whites, it is because they are drunk or afraid. Take away their fire-water and they find a natural pleasure in the murder of dove eyed babes and helpless women. Revenge has nothing to do with the present inhuman outrages. . . . Humanity demands the extermination of the blasted and besotted race."

Under the heading "What Shall Be Done with the Indians," the *Rochester Record* reprinted a column from the *St. Paul Press*. The author argued that a trial was not required because "There is no necessity whatever for carrying the forms of civilization into a war with the degraded savages who have made desolate hundreds of our happy frontier homes. . . . [and] the people of this state will never rest satisfied until the Indians are removed beyond our borders." A month later, the *Rochester Record* reprinted an article from the *St. Paul Union*, echoing Ramsey's words: "The people of this State do not consider this war over, and they will not until every Indian is either exterminated or removed beyond the borders of the State."

As the rumors spread through the region that the imprisoned Dakota men might not be executed, the anti-Dakota sentiment intensified. While Colonel Henry Sibley's forces were moving the men, "serious attack was made upon them with clubs and stones by the women and children [of the towns they passed]. One Indian had his jaw broken, and several others were severely injured. The women were quite determined to attack, and the soldiers had considerable troubles in repelling their assaults on the savages. The Indians were chained and comparably helpless. This is but the foretaste of what may be expected on the frontier." More than 1,600 Dakota men, women, and children were also incarcerated at Fort Snelling, where hundreds died due to the severe winter and poor conditions. The area below the fort, an institution of the US government, became a concentration camp: a place where noncombatants were confined without charges under harsh conditions.

Lieutenant O. P. Stearns, a lawyer and county attorney from Rochester who helped organize the Olmsted County Tigers, wrote to the *Rochester*

Republican in late December 1862 from Fort Ridgely. His comments express other worries and concerns. The men were restless and asked that books be sent to help them pass time. Stearns also implored citizens to look out for the families of the soldiers. He knew that when the draft was announced, some men had been induced to enlist by neighbors who promised to look out for their families in their absence, but took advantage and cheated them instead.

From September through November 1862, Colonel Sibley presided over the military tribunal deciding the destinies of more than four hundred Dakota men who were held prisoner in Mankato, Minnesota. In hasty trials, as many as forty-two in one day, the tribunal sentenced 303 of the men to death for murder and rape. The recommendation went to President Lincoln November 10, 1862. After reviewing all of the trial transcripts, the endorsements by Governor Ramsey and Major General John Pope, as well as the appeals for leniency expressed by Henry Whipple, the Episcopal bishop of Minnesota, who knew the Indian communities well, President Lincoln approved the execution of thirty-eight Dakota men. Soldiers of Minnesota regiments hanged these men in Mankato on December 26, 1862, in the largest mass execution ever held in the United States. Four thousand spectators gathered to watch. The men who were not executed were moved to a prison at Fort Davenport, Iowa, where they lived under death sentences until President Andrew Johnson ordered the remission of their sentences in 1866. Their families, carried by steamboats down the Mississippi and up the Missouri River, endured further starvation at Crow Creek before they were reunited. The Ho-Chunk, who had not participated in the war but resided on valuable agricultural land, were also sent to Crow Creek, their fourth forced relocation.

The US Congress passed acts removing the Dakota and Ho-Chunk from Minnesota in 1863. Well into 1863, various units continued to patrol the frontier regions. The Rochester Rangers were recognized for their bravery and "general good conduct upon the battlefield." A colonel issued a special order commending them for "following, overtaking, and slaughtering two Sioux Indians. . . . The rich reward of their energy and perseverance will be no doubt to stimulate other detachments to like earnestness." The Minnesota adjutant general's office offered a bounty on Dakota scalps until 1868.

Another crucial Rochester story was starting at this time. In 1862, Dr. William Worrall and Louise Mayo were living in Le Sueur, Minnesota, forty miles from the violence at New Ulm. William Worrall was a physician, and he headed for New Ulm to help care for the wounded,

I had not realized that men from Rochester went to fight the Dakota in 1862, and that calls for genocide raged in my community.

My great-grandparents were part of the wave of European immigrants coming to the United States in the 1850s. They were not the wealthy railroad, lumber, and land speculators who lobbied for removal of the Native Americans and promoted the settlements; they were the people who willingly benefited from that removal. They were greenhouse growers and craftsmen, people seeking opportunities for a more stable way of life than the one they came from. I understand that once they were in the United States, thrust into the political and cultural dynamics, these immigrants attempted to protect themselves and, in many cases, what little they had.

But to truly understand this war, people today must empathize with both sides simultaneously: the Dakota, enraged at seeing their lands taken, their children starving, and their very identity under attack, and the whites, enraged and terrified at the killings, concluding that the "Indians" must go. It's easy now to understand why the Dakota went to war. At that time, as a white person, I might have supported what we now call ethnic cleansing. I was deeply relieved to see that there are no Petersons listed among the men in the military units raised in 1862–63. Still, the raw hatred aimed at Indigenous people who were being unjustly removed from their homelands, subjected to broken promise after broken promise, and gradually exterminated through disease and starvation is a deeply disturbing and unavoidable part of my inheritance.

leaving Louise alone with their three young children. Although she was afraid, Louise took action to keep her family and community as safe as possible. She dressed in William's clothing and tucked her hair under a hat when she went to the barn. Then she organized the women in Le Sueur. They dressed up like men and brought any guns left in their homes—or other objects that from a distance might look like guns—and walked up and down the streets to give the appearance that there were still armed men in town.

Worried about her husband's well-being, Louise asked wounded refugees coming into Le Sueur, "Who dressed your wounds?" If they replied, "the Little Doctor," she knew her husband, who was short in stature, was still alive. She also took in people attempting to escape the violence. At one point, she had seven families staying in the house and three more families in the barn. She and her oldest daughter, Gertrude, worked day and night to feed them. One day they baked an entire barrel of flour into bread to feed their guests.

Although the Mayos had many positive interactions with Native Americans, before the war broke out, a Dakota man named Marpiya te najin (He Who Stands on a Cloud) had confronted William and threatened to take his horse one day when he was out making a house call. Louise remembered Marpiya te najin, also dubbed Cutnose by the white settlers, as one of "seven Indians who led the massacre, and who were hanged. . . . [I believe the] Government gave his body to The Doctor, and it was from that bad old Indian's skeleton that my boys got their first instruction in anatomy. It hung in their father's office for thirty years. Before they could whistle they had learned the name of every bone in the human make-up from that skeleton."

No record has been found showing that government agents gave William the body. Perhaps this transaction went unrecorded, a reward for his service in New Ulm; perhaps he, like other physicians, waited until nightfall and took the body from its shallow grave while officials turned their backs.

Months later, on April 24, 1863, Dr. Mayo was appointed by President Lincoln to be an examining surgeon for the Union Army in Rochester.

Marpiya te najin, about 1860. *MNHS*

Shortly thereafter, he opened an office that eventually evolved into Mayo Clinic, the internationally renowned health-care practice. Marpiya te najin's skull was held by the medical center until 1998, when it was returned to the Dakota people for burial. In 2018, Mayo Clinic administrators apologized, returned additional remains that might have been Marpiya te najin's, and established a scholarship in his name for Native American students in their education programs.

After the war, Minnesotans and others across the country provided an eager audience for stories about the atrocities committed by Dakota warriors; many narratives were sensationalized, exaggerated, and simply false, while others were accurate. A Rochester artist, John Stevens, found a way to profit from the stories of the war. The *Rochester Republican* announced that on October 6, 1862, Stevens, "who has for a long time been engaged in painting a panorama of this war, will exhibit the same to the citizens of this place and vicinity on Saturday evening. . . . We can safely recommend this painting for the painting it is—and not a single lantern humbug,—for we have seen it, and know it to be worthy the patronage of any community, as an artistic work, as well as a remembrance of the many blood-stained battle-fields where our brave boys fought."

Stevens was one of the first settlers to build a home and establish a business in Rochester. He painted signs and worked as an artist and photographer. After the war, Stevens became nationally known for creating panoramas documenting the US–Dakota War. His "Sioux War Panorama" consisted of thirty-six scenes painted on a canvas six feet wide and two hundred feet long. Billed as the "Most Extraordinary Exhibition in the World," representing the "Indian Massacre in Minnesota in 1862," Stevens's work was presented at opera houses and other performance venues throughout the Midwest. People living in the countryside, far away from the theaters and amusement venues popular in larger cities, were eager for entertainment. The images, story narration, and music combined in the moving panorama created a powerful, sensationalized performance.

OPERA HOUSE.

Thursday Evening, March 5th.

The Most Extraordinary Exhibition in the World!

STEVENS'
GREAT
TABLEAU PAINTINGS
REPRESENTING THE
INDIAN MASSACRE
IN MINNESOTA IN 1862.

THE GREAT MORAL EXHIBITION
OF THE AGE!

This is the most thrilling Exhibition ever offered to the public. It was commenced in 1862, and has been in steady progress until the present time, requiring a vast amount of labor. It was executed by that Celebrated Artist, JOHN STEVENS, who has visited the different localities, and taken many of the Sketches on the spot.

CAPT. C. E. SENCERBOX
Will delineate the different scenes.

Commencing with a Life-Like View of the North End of

LAKE SHETEK
Opening of the Outbreak of Aug. 20, 1862.

A View of the residence of Mr. Myers—Indians Destroying his Grain, &c.
A View of the house of Mr. Hurd—Shooting of Mr. Voight—Flight of Mrs. Hurd and Children, &c.
Interior View of Mr. Hurd's Residence—Indians Destroying its contents.

House of Mr. Cook, a Beautiful Landscape Scene.
Murder of Mr. Cook and capture of his Wife—Thrilling narrative of her sufferings.

CHARLES HATCH Bringing NEWS OF THE OUTBREAK to the Settlers!

Flight of the Eastlick Family and other Settlers in a wagon—Men armed and covering their retreat, Indians mounted and in pursuit—Women abandon the wagon —Battle with the Indians—Slaughter of nearly all the male portion of the Settlers —Capture of the Women—Old Women and Children Killed.

FLIGHT OF THE NOBLE BOY, MURTON EASTLICK!

With his Infant Brother, 18 months old, in his arms, whom he carries 52 miles to a place of safety.

ESCAPE OF MRS. EASTLICK!
And a Graphic Description of her Sufferings, etc.

WAR DANCE, AT NIGHT.
Indians showing in pantomine the struggles and contortions of their victims of the day before.

PORTRAITS

Of LITTLE HILL, Winnebago Chief. KOZE BOSH, one of the principal Actors in the great Massacre, the Indian that captured Mrs. Cook. MRS. COOK in her Indian Costume. OTHER DAY, a friendly Chief that saved 62 Whites. RED IRON, friendly Sioux, that delivered the captives to Gen. Sibley at Camp Release. NEH QUASH and WA-KE-TIK, or FLYING SKY. Also Portraits of nearly every Indian Chief that was engaged in the Massacre.

FULL LENGTH PORTRAIT OF GENERAL SIBLEY.

Grand and Imposing Spectacle, A Bird's-Eye View of NEW-ULM!

VIEW OF THE FALLS OF ST. ANTHONY.

THRILLING SCENES!

Killing of Captain Dodd, in the Attack on New Ulm. Indian Attack on a party engaged in thrashing near St. Peter—Massacre of the men and capturing horses. Killing of Mrs. Smith and daughter by Chief Rattling Runner. Murder of 18 Women and Children in a wagon, by CUT NOSE. A FULL LENGTH PORTRAIT of this Demon.

CHASKA,	OLD BETS,
The Murderer of George Gleason, and Capturer of the Wakefield Family.	A great favorite with both Whites and Indians.

View of Camp Release. Surrender of the Female Captives to Gen. Sibley by Red Iron.
Hanging of 38 Indians at Mankato. View of a portion of the City of Mankato.

Tickets 50 cts. Reserved Seats 25 cts. extra.

For sale at Munger Bros. Music Store, on Thursday morning, at 9 o'clock.
Doors open in the Evening at 7 o'clock. To commence at 8 o'clock precisely.

St. Paul Press Print.

A playbill for Stevens's panorama, about 1873. *MNHS*

Like popular panoramas of the Mississippi River painted in the 1840s and 1850s, Stevens's presentations consisted of a canvas rolled onto a large dowel and placed into a wood frame. A "crankist" would advance the roll, scene by scene, backlit with kerosene lamps, while a narrator—often Stevens—told the story. The painted scenes moved across the stage, sometimes accompanied by music played by a violinist or string ensemble, creating a dramatic portrayal of the events.

Stevens heard stories from white settlers who fled to Rochester to escape the violence, including Lavina Eastlick, whom he met on a stagecoach. Lavina's husband, John, and three of their sons were killed by the Dakota near their home at Lake Shetek on August 19. She was injured

Panel depicting "Slaughter Slough" from Stevens's "Panorama of the Indians Massacre of 1862 and the Black Hills"; oil, created about 1865. *Gilcrease Museum, Tulsa, Oklahoma*

and left for dead, while her eleven-year-old son, Merton, escaped with his toddler brother and a gravely injured neighbor. When the neighbor was unable to continue, Merton went on alone for fifty miles, barefoot, carrying his little brother on his back, until they reached a road, where the postal carrier covering the Sioux Falls–New Ulm route came upon them. Lavina staggered out of the embattled area having survived her injuries and was reunited with her sons. Merton became well known as the Boy Hero of the Indian Massacre.

John Stevens included the Eastlick story along with others in his panorama. Lavina and Merton stayed in Rochester for a while. When they occasionally attended the panorama exhibitions, their presence drew crowds, and Stevens shared the proceeds with them. One historian of the time noted that the Stevens panorama provided "life-size pictures that by the liberal use of red paint fully displayed the blood-thirstiness of the savages."

The scenes and narrative revealed the gruesome deaths of men, women, and children who were shot, stabbed, or bludgeoned by the Dakota. One panel revealed powerful and dignified portraits of President Lincoln and his cabinet. Another panel depicted the execution of the thirty-eight Dakota men in Mankato. Portraits of the Dakota leaders portray them as shifty and disheveled. There are no panels depicting the Dakota and their way of life before the Europeans arrived. There are no panels of the Dakota starving. There are no panels of the settlers or militia killing the Dakota. There are no panels of the corrupt officials of the Office of Indian Affairs or the clerks who denied the Dakota food.

Eventually, Lavina Eastlick resettled in the Mankato area and published a booklet of her recollections of the attack on her family. Merton returned to Rochester when he married a woman from the city. He worked with John Stevens and as a carpenter until he died in 1875 at age twenty-four of a pulmonary condition. Unable to afford a gravestone, his family buried his body in an unmarked grave in Oakwood Cemetery in Rochester. Stevens continued without Merton, creating at least four panoramas of the US–Dakota War. In addition to displaying them at opera houses in

Rochester, he toured with them for several years in a rig decorated with a colorful canvas promoting the show.

The enthusiastic reception of the biased and sensationalized performances was not limited to the years shortly after the war. In 1921, one of the panoramas was displayed at the Metropolitan Opera House. When the tone became too somber during the presentation, the narrator pretended to mix up his lines, "to give the necessary humorous touch to an otherwise tragic subject." The *Rochester Daily Bulletin* commented that the "paintings represent a vivid account . . . of the dastardly outrages of those early days." In November 1927, under the headline "Fearful Massacre, Bloody Scenes, Revealed in Thrilling Panorama," the *Rochester Post Bulletin* reported that workmen renovating a building in town uncovered an old billboard promoting the exhibition: "Murder of Mr. Cook and capture of his wife, thrilling tales of suffering. . . . Murder of 18 women and children in a wagon by Cut Nose. A full portrait of this demon. Hanging of 38 Indians at Mankato. Admission 25 cents. Children 15 cents. A grand benefit for the school children in the afternoon."

The First National Bank planned to display the billboard in their window "so that all interested parties" could see it. After being displayed, the bank intended to give the billboard to the Olmsted County Historical Society. Later that month, the newspaper began printing a serialized version of Lavina Eastlick's memoir, "Thrilling Incidents of the Indian War of 1862 . . . a narrative of the Outrages and Horrors witnessed by Mrs. L. Eastlick." The panoramas were pulled out repeatedly until the 1950s. In retelling the stories of savagery and ignoring the causes of the war, descendants of the settlers were, in effect, justifying taking the land and creating a one-sided narrative that endured.

The panoramas were criticized for perhaps the first time when they were shown at the Minneapolis Institute of Art in 1949 and considered prejudiced. The showing ended early, and the canvas rolls were returned to the Minnesota Historical Society. That same year, an article in the *Rochester Post Bulletin* described the gravestone that the Olmsted County Historical Society placed on Merton Eastlick's grave: "Boy Hero—Indian Massacre—Marker placed by Olmsted County Historical

Society." The article quotes his mother: "The odds were fearfully against us. 200 Indians against six white men."

The following year, in 1950, the *Rochester Post Bulletin* announced in a headline "Massacre Scene Showing Set for Art Festival Here." A Rochester attorney who had purchased another of the Stevens panoramas for twenty-five dollars from "a family of colored entertainers" in Winona, Minnesota, and gifted it to the Minnesota Historical Society said, "I saw it as a boy and I still retain a very vivid impression which it gave me as a child, of Indian frightfulness." Images of the scenes in the panoramas appeared on a national scale in a 1959 issue of *Life* magazine as a part of a series of articles on "How the West Was Won: Cowboy Days, the Indian Wars."

Local attitudes about Native Americans ranging from hatred to silence lasting for a century and a half may explain the small size of the Native community in Rochester and continued misunderstandings.

Questioning the presence and significance of the Dakota people in the Rochester area resurfaced in the last decade. In 2010, in the midst of the conflict between mountain bikers proposing a system of trails in Indian Heights Park and residents opposed to the potential damage to habitat and quiet recreation, the presence of the Dakota people and the burials on the bluff came to light. Not everyone believed the claim that the bluff was a burial site and therefore protected from development by state law. The state archaeologist and the Minnesota Indian Affairs Council began planning a survey to authenticate the burial ground. The Dakota participants then expressed their preference not to pursue official authentication of the site, because such a study would require disturbing the graves. Although several histories written by white settlers and Dakota oral narratives confirm that the burials occurred, many people wondered why no physical evidence of them survived.

Marion Sloan's reminiscences, recorded in 1937 and archived at the History Center of Olmsted County, provide the answer. She had seen the Dakota graves as a child, probably within ten years of the burials, and she described them in detail.

[They were] shallow and covered with rough boards split by hand from logs and shaped like a low roof resting on the ground. The graves were quite close together in a row from east to west. We, although half frightened, could peep through the cracks and catch glances of the dusky forms wrapped in their blankets with trinkets and hunting implements by their side. . . . At the time of the New Ulm Massacre feeling was very strong against the Indian. Boys and young men from town went out to the burial ground and destroyed the graves, taking the trinkets and implements and scattering bones over the hillside. I remember seeing a skull on top of a young sapling.

Sloan's account of the destruction of the graves is perhaps more believable than a theory repeated during the park board debate in 2010 that the cyclone that tore through town in 1883 had blown the graves away.

After months of hearings and heated debates, in 2011, the Rochester Park Board decided to prohibit mountain bike use in the park and to recognize the historical Native American presence on the land. The

Peter Lengkeek at Indian Heights Park, Healing and Reconciliation Ceremony, April 2012. *Diversity Foundation, Inc.*

following spring, in April 2012, Peter Lengkeek, also known as Two Arrows and a leader on the Crow Creek Reservation, stood at Indian Heights Park and shared the story of his great-great-grandmother, who was one of the Dakota people removed from the Rochester area. He told the small group gathered at Indian Heights Park for a blessing and reconciliation ceremony that Rose died of starvation shortly after completing the four-hundred-mile journey to Crow Creek Reservation. He heard the story from his grandmother, Rose's granddaughter. Dakota oral histories and journals written by the soldiers and missionaries who accompanied them on their forced walk describe how the women saved their culture through their strength and resilience. They endured starvation and rape during the relocation, resorting to scavenging grains from livestock feces and prostituting themselves to survive and provide for their families.

At Crow Creek, the Dakota continued to endure abuse; their children were later taken to boarding schools that attempted to erase their language and culture. Lengkeek explained that the Dakota persevered, although the trauma has been inherited by all generations who follow.

Standing before the white and Native people at Indian Heights that day, Lengkeek acknowledged that these wrongs of the past cannot be undone, but he generously suggested that they can be put behind us, and we can go forward in a spirit of healing and reconciliation. He explained that the word *Dakota* means "in harmony, to be friends." The Dakota are people of love and compassion, not like the warriors portrayed in American Western movies, an image they have had to endure for decades and which caused many to hide their identities. After singing a creation prayer, Lengkeek noted that federal regulations prohibited Native religious practices, including prayers, sweat lodges, and powwows, until 1978. The United States was so intent on destroying Indigenous cultures that every effort was made to fully repress all expressions of Dakota life.

The Native Americans who had gathered for the ceremony that day at Indian Heights Park gave the mayor of Rochester a star quilt with bold green patches forming tipis and stars on a white fabric background.

Each stitch was sewn by women with a prayer for good health and happiness. The moving event closed with calls for reconciliation from another elder who envisioned building a bridge based on mutual understanding, enrichment, and respect.

The Dakota and Ho-Chunk people did not just walk away from the Wazi Ozu Wakpa in search of a better place to live, as the written histories imply. They were forcibly removed. The Rochester Rangers militia spent a year "protecting" the area around Fort Ripley and assisted with the exile of the Dakota. Subsequently, they finished their three-year enlistment fighting for the Union in the Civil War. Many were discharged due to disability. Several died on battlefields. A few were taken prisoner and kept in camps, including the infamous Andersonville military prison for Union soldiers. They were brave men who made sacrifices to protect what they felt was their land and way of life, but in doing so, they evicted the Dakota people from the land and the lifestyle they deserved.

The hatred of Indigenous peoples in the early years of the Rochester community slipped into a long period of silence, nearly erasing the presence of the Dakota people and their way of life. A small Native American community resists this erasure, and it is long overdue that Rochester residents support and celebrate their presence. One example of recent acts of healing and reconciliation was Mayo Clinic's distribution of COVID-19 testing resources in 2020 to eleven reservations in need. The clinic also facilitated the care of people testing positive, transferring patients to Rochester, where they were welcomed by an employee of Dakota and Ho-Chunk descent, Valerie Guimaraes. She ensured their cultural practices could be respected during their treatment, including the burning of sage or sweetgrass, a practice known as smudging. Continued commitment by the Rochester community to understand and respect Dakota and Ho-Chunk values and traditions has mutually beneficial potential for both communities.

CHAPTER 2

Waterways, Roadways, and Railways to Development

The most visible mode of transportation connecting Rochester with the rest of the world is a busy four-lane section of Highway 52 that extends between Rochester and the Twin Cities of Minneapolis and St. Paul. The ninety-mile trip takes a little over an hour by car. But few people know that this main artery began as the Dubuque Trail, a stagecoach route covering the 240 miles between St. Paul, Minnesota, and Dubuque, Iowa. Rochester was a stop along the way.

Marker for the Dubuque Trail, in the 700 block of Third Avenue Southeast. *Photo by Brendan Bush*

When Minnesota became a US territory in 1849, fewer than five thousand European Americans lived in the region. Less than a decade later, in 1858, when Minnesota attained statehood, it was home to 170,000 residents, including immigrants who took claims in the southeast corner of the new state, dubbed the "Minnesota Triangle" by historian Arthur Larsen. The region, bordered by the Mississippi River on the east and the Minnesota and Blue Earth Rivers north of Iowa, consists of karst geology, rich with limestone, caves, and springs. Larsen reflected the speed of white settlement: "Towns sprang into existence where but a few months before there had been virgin wilderness. The forest melted away and houses showed through the tangled undergrowth wherever a wearied idealist had found his Eden."

Stagecoaches and roads had replaced canoes and waterways as primary routes of movement. The newcomers used the paths made by Native Americans and fur traders to find their way inland. The ability to transport people and mail throughout the region, and especially to and from the growing commercial center of St. Paul, was a priority; however, the new territorial government did not have funding for the project, and it appealed to Congress for assistance. Representatives from other states argued that they had already invested a large sum in the region through the treaties of 1851. Henry Sibley, a fur trader and the Minnesota Territory's first representative, argued that the federal government would not be able to profit from settlement of the area if people could not get to it. To further his argument, despite his Dakota business associations and friendships, he claimed that Minnesota was "inhabited by the largest and most warlike tribes on the North American continent." A road system would allow troops to quickly suppress a violent conflict with the Indians. Sibley's anti-Indian fearmongering was successful in combination with the desires of businessmen and legislators to realize economic returns. The federal government, along with the Minnesota territorial and state governments, funded road development in the 1850s. Sibley became Minnesota's first state governor—and later led the military forces in the US–Dakota War of 1862.

Oxen pulling wagons on Broadway, 1865. *HCOC*

A web of stagecoach routes eventually crisscrossed the southeastern Minnesota Triangle, fueling growth to the region. George and Henrietta Head were among the first to arrive in July 1854, traveling from Wisconsin and settling along the south branch of the Zumbro River. They jumped a claim made on the land before they arrived, but they later bought out the original owners. George dragged a log behind oxen to create the first road for the new town. Henrietta proudly rode down the new street, soon to be known as Broadway, sidesaddle on a horse. They named their riverbank claim Rochester because the falls reminded George of the Genesee River Falls in Rochester, New York, his boyhood home. The comparison of the falls might have been exaggerated, perhaps to promote his new investment. George Head had come into Minnesota Territory to pursue a career in real estate, after having been a deputy sheriff and a baker in Watertown, Wisconsin.

The common belief that Rochester, New York, was named for the town of Rochester in Kent, England, was recently debunked by a writer for the *Rochester Post Bulletin*. Instead, it was named after Nathaniel Rochester, a member of the North Carolina militia during the Revolutionary War and a successful businessman. He became a land speculator and in 1803 purchased land on Lake Ontario near the Genesee River, where he and other investors developed the town, first incorporated in 1817 as Rochesterville, later Rochester, New York. His account ledgers, now in the possession of the University of Rochester, clearly document that Nathaniel Rochester owned enslaved people; he bought and sold human beings and separated families. Indirectly, Rochester, Minnesota, is named for a slave owner.

In addition to the government funding, businesses and investors financed the road expansions, speculating on the development of the region. Roads were imperative for marketing produce, for mail service at all times of the year, and for adequate stagecoach service. The ability to connect the steamboat lines running along the rivers with the stagecoaches using the new road system sped growth in the Triangle, with Rochester in the center.

Also in 1854, the first stagecoach came south through Rochester from St. Paul. Shortly, another coach route was established, east to west, from Winona to Mankato. The crossroads of the stagecoach routes created a location ripe for a growing hospitality industry, consisting of hotels and taverns. The Heads built a log shanty that became known as Head's Tavern; people today who cross the bridge at Fourth Street Southeast travel directly past the spot. Soon other proprietors built the Broadway House, Cook House, and Bradley House to serve travelers and newcomers.

Even with improved roadways, such as they were, stagecoach travel through the area was rough. Two or four horses pulled a coach; sometimes oxen were used. Other times, passengers sat on seats made of boards nailed across the wagon bed. The rigor of these journeys was described by Amelia Ullmann, who left St. Paul on St. Patrick's Day in 1857 for Dubuque, accompanying her husband on a business trip. He was "aghast" when she said she wanted to make the trip with him, claiming "it is impossible for a woman to make such a trip . . . men make it with fear and dread." Despite her husband's offer of one hundred dollars for a new fur coat to urge her to stay home, Amelia persevered. They boarded a US mail coach, which often carried passengers in addition to the mail. In the winter months, the coaches were sleds. The only amenity provided to passengers was straw in the wagon bed; they needed to carry their own food and blankets. She packed a bag with several roasted fowls and wine, and a trunk with clothing. Two hours after their departure, dark clouds filled the sky, and they were in a "dense, driving snow that cut off the sight of everything beyond a few feet of the sledge." The horses and driver "found their way by a sort of instinct; for there was nothing so far as we could see in the darkness of the storm." The sled overturned several times, causing the horses to flounder through the shoulder-high snow. The canvas cover did not protect the passengers from snow pelting their faces. The journey from St. Paul to Dubuque took a week, with Rochester as one of the stops along the way.

In 1857, a writer for the *St. Paul Advertiser* noted that in summer, "Rochester is a sort of grand encampment for the meeting streams of emigration. . . . We counted one hundred emigrant wagons last summer on the outskirts of town, their occupants huddled in groups around a dozen or more fires." In the short six years after the opening of the Dubuque Trail, the city emerged as the business hub of the Triangle and home to 1,424 settlers.

Although the stagecoaches and overland travel began to replace waterways as conduits of transportation in the area, the Zumbro River became critical to Rochester's growth in the early years. The river was first named Wazi Ozu Wakpa ("river where the pines grow") by the Dakota and later Rivière des Embarras ("river of obstructions or difficulties") by French traders. The name originated because canoes frequently became snagged by trees felled by pervasive erosion. Despite the obstructions, the sixty-five-mile tributary provided a route that was often easier to travel than overland through forested areas, and the river provided travelers with water and food in the form of fish, birds, herds of bison, and other mammals coming to the riverbanks for water.

The Zumbro River's role in Rochester's growth shifted from being a transportation conduit to powering the milling industry, a surprising source of economic growth for a town that later became a medical mecca. Various types of mills, driven by the river's current and falls, supported building and provided jobs, capitalizing on the growing agriculture surrounding the city. Joseph Alexander, who arrived in the area shortly after George and Henrietta Head, spurred growth by building a sawmill that could produce five hundred feet of lumber a day. Frederick A. Olds opened a wheat flouring mill in 1856. Joseph Alexander also owned and operated a woolen mill that provided a market for fleece obtained from farmers raising sheep in the area. Another business, the Rochester Woolen Mills, opened in 1897 and was featured in *Northwestern Magazine* in 1901, with photos of its wool sorting and sewing rooms.

The grist mills converted from grindstones to roller mills around 1905 and turned out between two hundred and six hundred barrels of

Women sewing at the Rochester Woolen Manufacturing Company, as featured in the *Northwestern Magazine*, May 1901. *HCOC*

flour a day with the names Snow Flake Flour, Graham Flour, and Buckwheat Flour. They also made Royal Breakfast Food. General Mills, a large milling, flour, and food production company in Minneapolis, leased property along the Zumbro River in the 1930s. They opened a Farm Services Store and a Red Owl grocery store, both business chains affiliated with the milling giant. The president of General Mills may have been encouraged to expand into Rochester because of his friendship with the Mayo family.

While the Zumbro River made these mills possible, its meandering route and minimal falls resulted in insufficient water velocity for optimal milling. Mill owners initiated the first alterations in the path and flow of the river, actions that later may have had repercussions. To increase water speed, mill races—ditches running alongside the river—were created.

The J. A. Cole Milling Company in Rochester, 1912. *HCOC*

One mill race was fifteen feet deep and ran three blocks, carrying water from Strawberry Dam, named for the proliferation of strawberries surrounding the pond, to a second dam at the other end of the race, forming Mill Pond. In addition to increasing the productivity of the mill, the ponds created picturesque opportunities for fishing and picnicking in the summer and ice skating in the winter.

Although some residents perceived the mill ponds as pastoral respites, depending on the time of year they could also be eyesores holding stagnant, mucky water and emitting unpleasant odors. In 1897, city officials considered the possibility of building a larger dam on the Zumbro that would create a lake to replace the sometimes smelly, undesirable mill pond. The proposal became controversial when Dr. William Worrall Mayo proposed a location for the dam that would make his farm lakefront property. Officials deferred the decision, and conversations and debates continued until after Dr. W. W. Mayo's death in 1911. It was not until 1930 that the city made plans to create a lake by damming the Zumbro River near its convergence with Silver Creek, replacing one of the large mill ponds.

Olmsted County was one of just four of Minnesota's eighty-seven counties that lacked a natural lake. The Great Depression was in full swing; 1,500 men in Rochester needed jobs badly. Funding from the federal Civil Works Administration (CWA) and Works Progress Administration (WPA) funded the development of the lake in 1934–35. Eight hundred men with shovels and mules dug the lake's basin, converting a poor pasture and gravel and sand pits into a fine recreational park.

On June 24, 1937, Silver Lake was dedicated with a daylong celebration featuring picnics, events for children, sing-alongs, and fireworks. The front of the program was decorated with a drawing of the lake with geese and canoes. The back included a drawing of a log cabin, a canoe, a tipi, and two Native Americans—another example of the romanticization of Indigenous people, who had been exiled from the area. In 1938, when President Franklin D. Roosevelt was in Rochester to visit his son James during his treatment at Saint Marys Hospital, proud city leaders toured the president around the lake in his car.

In 1949, a coal power plant built along Silver Lake began operation. The plant discharged warm water into the lake, preventing it from freezing over and creating a year-round home for Canada geese. The geese originated from a small flock Dr. Charles Mayo (known as Dr. Charlie), son of Dr. W. W. Mayo, had acquired in 1924 for the pond at Mayowood, the home he and his wife, Edith, had built outside of town. Some of Dr. Mayo's geese relocated to Silver Lake after it was built, and by 1959, when the Zumbro Valley Audubon Society held its first Christmas Bird Count, they found 2,100 geese in the Rochester area, most of them at Silver Lake. The year-round flock grew to over 20,000 birds in the 1970s and '80s, along with some mallards and swans. The population peaked at 33,000 in 1998. Their presence had become a part of the city's identity—and yet, to some, the geese were a messy nuisance and health hazard when their droppings covered playground areas and walking and biking paths.

In an effort to deter geese, in 2007 the park board removed feeders and planted tall native plants at the edge of the lake. But eventually, the population started to increase again, and in 2017, it reached an eight-year record of 9,884 geese, causing the city to prohibit feeding them, a popular activity for families and visitors. By spring 2020, a nearby beach had to be closed because of high levels of bacteria in the water, causing intensified concern. In response, the city initiated a new plan for controlling the goose population that aroused controversy. In 2021, the Rochester Parks and Recreation department proposed addling eggs—coating fertilized eggs in vegetable oil—which halts development of the embryo and reduces the goose population. If eggs are merely removed from nests, the geese will lay more. Some residents opposed addling eggs on a humanitarian basis. Some residents did not see a need to reduce the goose population. A state senator threatened to suspend egg addling through an amendment on a bill before the state legislature. He advocated for expanding the hunting season or catching the geese with nets instead of addling eggs. Ultimately, 314 eggs from sixty-five nests were treated by addling.

Despite the controversy, the Canada goose remains an icon in the city. In 2009, a public art project resulted in eighteen five-foot whimsically decorated goose statues, which are positioned throughout downtown. A popular restaurant across from Mayo Clinic's Saint Marys Hospital is called the Canadian Honker. The city baseball team is named the Rochester Honkers. The geese, in one form or another, appear to be a permanent fixture in the city.

While Rochester benefited by being at the confluence of the south branch of the Zumbro River and the Silver, Cascade, and Bear Creeks, this network of waterways could be immensely destructive. After George and Henrietta Head's arrival in 1854, the south branch of the Zumbro River flooded in 1855, 1859, 1866, 1882, 1903, 1908, 1925, 1933, 1942, 1951, 1952, 1954, 1958, 1961, 1962, 1965, 1966 (twice), 1967 (twice), 1969, 1973, 1974, 1978, 1986, 2018, and 2019, washing out roads, destroying businesses and homes, and occasionally taking lives.

On June 23, 1908, after a night of heavy rain, the river rose four feet. Five hundred head of hogs perished, and an approach to a bridge was

Rochester in flood, July 6, 1978, looking west along Fourth Street Southeast. The Plummer Building, with the Mayo Building behind it, is at upper right. *MNHS*

washed out. Many people were dangerously stranded, including the Cole family. The three young children and their parents first escaped to a roof, and then rising waters led them to climb onto a tree, where they hung on for four hours until they were rescued by boat. The newspaper that day was printed by hand because of a power outage. On June 4, 1942, sixteen-year-old Willard Marek was swept into the "swirling, muddy current" and drowned while riding his bike after a torrential rain sent Cascade Creek "on its greatest rampage in recent history," as the *Post Bulletin* put it. A flood destroyed nine hundred homes and businesses in 1951. In 1962 and 1965, the river flooded in the unlikely month of March, when the spring snow melt, complicated by ice jams, caused the water to rise.

The worst flood occurred July 5 and 6, 1978, when the mighty Zumbro rose to its highest known level, eleven feet over flood stage. A malfunctioning elevator in a long-term care facility took four residents and one staff member down into the floodwater, drowning all five. Five thousand homes were evacuated, and the Red Cross assisted 14,000 people with food, housing, and cleaning supplies.

The 1978 flood bolstered plans that had been in the works for several years, for a project intended to keep the Zumbro River and the streams within its banks. The city and federal government provided $155 million to build seven reservoirs, dredge Silver Lake, replace three bridges, and widen and deepen the river in some places. The work was accomplished between 1988 and 1990 and resulted in new recreational areas and walking and bike paths. Subsequently, flooding in Rochester has primarily been limited to roads and parks, including in 2019, when the area experienced a record-breaking annual total of 50.6 inches of precipitation.

While the flood project served its intended purpose, the new concrete walls winding through town that prevented flooding also deterred business development along the river. In the fall of 2021, the Destination Medical Center (DMC) collaborative initiative, funded with government and private dollars, held its annual meeting in a parking lot along the river on property that was once part of Frederick Olds's milling operation and near the place George and Henrietta Head created the first road, Broadway. The DMC and local businesses committed to rebuilding along the river in hopes of drawing people back to its banks to live, work, and recreate.

Migration to Rochester accelerated beyond the access provided by waterways and stagecoach lines on October 12, 1864, when the Winona & St. Peter Railroad connected the growing town to Winona, Minnesota, along the Mississippi River and St. Peter in central Minnesota. Powered by a wood-fueled steam engine, the train took three and a half hours to navigate the steep hills between Winona and Rochester and travel what later became a forty-five-minute trip by car. The progress was not easy. As the crew was in the process of putting down the last miles of track in northwest Rochester, one of the property owners, an early settler in the area, confronted the grading foreman, who shot the Rochester resident in a scuffle. The foreman was quickly hurried out of town as a crowd formed, threatening to lynch him. The Rochester resident survived his injuries, and the railroad became a reality.

The independent rail service soon became part of the Chicago & North Western Railroad, followed by the Winona & Southwestern Railroad, and later the Chicago Great Western Railway. The primary cargo was wheat from the surrounding fields headed to larger markets, followed by retail merchandise, butter, hides, barley, and lumber. The first train station built in Rochester in 1865 compared favorably in its decor to depots farther east. Its waiting room was large, comfortable, and well lit. Passenger traffic continued at a steady pace as the town grew.

The Mayos knew that an effective transportation system was crucial for the growth of their medical practice. The buggies coming to town were slow, and many patients could not stand the jarring ride. As the clinic's national reputation grew, the railroads serving Rochester recognized their role in transporting ill and injured people, a new initiative nationwide. Trains stored medical chests with emergency supplies, and staff were trained to "check hemorrhage, administer opiates for pain and stimulants for shock, and apply temporary antiseptic dressings," according to Helen Clapesattle, an early historian of Mayo Clinic.

In 1892, a train traveling through Chicago hit two women riding in a buggy. One woman was unconscious and bleeding from the nose, mouth, and ear. She was put on the train, and the conductor headed full speed for Rochester. At Saint Marys Hospital, Dr. Charlie Mayo opened a fissure in her skull and stopped the bleeding. Another patient, a seventeen-year-old girl living on a farm forty miles from Rochester, was badly burned when a kerosene lamp exploded. Her family and friends carried her on a gurney for twenty-five miles to the nearest train station because she could not endure the pain of a bumpy carriage ride. A train from St. Charles brought her the rest of the way to Rochester.

The Mayos themselves benefited from the swift and effective rail system in 1911, when Dr. Charlie Mayo became seriously ill in New York City on his way home from a surgical association meeting. After a procedure by local surgeons failed, Dr. Charlie's condition worsened. His brother,

Dr. Will, and their highly skilled anesthetist Florence Henderson caught a train in Rochester intending to get to Dr. Charlie as soon as possible. When they arrived in Winona, an express train was waiting for them. The railroad broke all records in delivering Dr. Will and Florence Henderson to New York. Freight trains were shunted to sidings and passengers had to wait while "Dr. Mayo's train" sped by on cleared tracks. Dr. Will arrived in time to save his brother's life by operating to remove his gallbladder.

Rail service to Rochester was provided by various small railway companies that over time were bought out by larger ones, resulting in most service to the city being provided by the Chicago Great Western Railway with its Bluebird and Redbird lines between the Twin Cities and other towns in southeastern Minnesota and the Chicago & North Western Railroad.

Perhaps one of the best-known lines was the Rochester Special line, consisting of cars designed to accommodate patients and visitors going to Mayo Clinic. Beginning service in 1930, the Chicago & North Western Railway brochure boasted "travel perfection. . . . Viewed with imagination, insight, and a sense of beauty, railway equipment has become an epic enterprise, as thrilling as any spectacle in this period of advancing progress." Multiple cars provided luxurious lounges, including a sun parlor with wicker chairs, light buff shades, and decor in refreshing tones of rose, amber, and blue. An ornamental frieze and leather chairs with walnut molding enriched the observation lounge. The homey atmosphere included a writing desk and lighting fixtures with a chandelier flame design.

In addition to providing comfort, some of the cars were specially designed to accommodate patients boarding in wheelchairs and on stretchers. The standard doors at the ends of the cars were supplemented by three side doors that allowed easier access for wheelchairs and stretchers. According to the brochure, the beds, "possessing the resilient buoyancy of finely tempered coil springs," were also wider than standard. Roller bearings on the train ensured a smoother ride, and heavy rubber inserts, installed above and below the truck equalizer springs, reduced rail and friction noise. In essence, the Rochester Special was a hospital train line. One of the Rochester Special cars was named after Joseph Lister, a renowned British surgeon known for creating methods for reducing surgical infections, and the other for Ephraim McDowell, an admired eighteenth-century American physician. They carried the everyday patients to Rochester, and they carried famous patients, too, including James Roosevelt, son of President Franklin and Eleanor Roosevelt, and the body of Minnesota governor John A. Johnson, who died after surgery at Mayo Clinic on September 21, 1909.

In 1934, the Chicago & North Western Railway upgraded its service when it replaced its steam engines with faster diesel-powered engines. Several new "400" lines began connecting Chicago and the Twin Cities of Minneapolis and St. Paul. The 400 was named for its ability to go

On September 4, 1939, *Life* magazine featured the "Joseph Lister Ambulance Pullman Train" in an article about the wonders of the Mayo Clinic. *Rochester Public Library*

The "hospital train" from Chicago carries a special Pullman, Joseph Lister, with wide doors for stretcher cases.

four hundred miles in four hundred minutes. In 1936, the Minnesota 400 line began service from Mankato to Chicago, via a connection in Wyeville, Wisconsin. This route stopped in Rochester, providing the city with new, faster service to Chicago. Between 1936 and 1963, Rochester was served at different times by three lines of the Chicago & North Western Railroad: the Minnesota 400, the Dakota 400, and the Rochester 400.

In addition to providing comfortable transport on the trains, the Chicago & North Western passenger station in Chicago also supported traveling patients by including a pharmacy and hospital in the terminal. Day and night nurses staffed the hospital and sick room. Comfort for the journey, especially for fragile patients, was important. Mayo staff were assigned to meet all trains coming into town and assist in efficiently transporting patients to the clinic or one of the hospitals by ambulance.

Three decades after trains began providing transportation in the Rochester area, automobiles came on the scene. The first horseless carriage in Rochester, powered by a 1.5-horsepower engine, appeared on August 31, 1898. A visitor from Spring Valley, Minnesota, a town south of Rochester, attracted a large crowd when he parked the vehicle downtown on Broadway. The twenty-eight-mile trip took him two hours and fifteen minutes, a route that fifty years later could be driven in under thirty minutes. Dr. Charlie Mayo, who had a special interest in most things mechanical, came out of his office to look at it. In January 1900, he acquired a carriage with a steam-driven four-horsepower engine, which allowed him to travel twenty-five miles an hour. The introduction of the car in town was controversial. The loud noise automobiles made frightened horses. Initially, the advantages over horses were slim because the roads were poor—mud and snow could easily cause the early autos to become stuck. The tires were not resilient, and early headlights were not very effective, making travel at night and in the winter difficult.

By 1908, there were fifty cars in Rochester, and by 1912, there were enough owners to form the Rochester Auto Club. Packard, Maxwell, Knox, Brush, and Buick were among the favored brands. By 1916, there were a thousand cars in Olmsted County, one for every twenty-seven persons. The first lighted "stop and go" sign was erected on Broadway in 1920. The police had to operate it, but it seemed to simplify the regulation of traffic, at least when drivers understood it.

Almost as soon as the car came to town, parking became an issue. One early debate was about parking parallel rather than diagonal. In 1940, the city attempted to address a shortage of parking by installing parking meters in hopes of keeping the available parking space "fluid." In 1946, a city leader noted that "there is only so much room available for parking" regardless of parallel or diagonal approaches. He insisted that the city acquire land for off-street parking, and thus parking lots were born, followed soon after by a parking ramp. Parking shortages continued to plague Rochester even after several ramps were built. At some point, Mayo Clinic began requiring employees to park off campus and shuttled them to their work locations downtown. In 2019, the city raised the monthly parking rates to $154 a month and had plans to raise them to well over $200 a month in order to encourage commuters to use public transportation. When the pandemic hit in 2020, employees everywhere who could fulfill their work responsibilities remotely began working at home—at the kitchen table, in a bedroom, in the basement. The impact of the pandemic alone appeared to have abated the century-old parking dilemmas in Rochester. At least for a while.

As cars became more popular, airplanes also emerged as a new form of transportation. Eight years after the Wright brothers launched their first flight, a plane landed in Rochester. In 1911, two wheat farmers from North Dakota were invited to town by Arthur Ellis, Dr. Christopher Graham's chauffeur. Dr. Graham was one of the early members of the Mayo practice, and Ellis was an organizing member of the Rochester Model Aeroplane Club. Dr. Graham bought flat land southeast of

Diagonal parking on Second Street Southwest with the Mayo Clinic building
(now Plummer Building), 1931. *HCOC*

downtown that made a reasonable landing field for planes. In addition to the model plane enthusiasts, the William T. McCoy American Legion Post 92 advocated for aviation in Rochester, but it wasn't until after World War I that planes became more prevalent, when five sons of the Furlow family returned from serving in the war. Four of them had been involved in aviation, two of them as pilots. They were eager to begin air mail service to Rochester. In 1928, the first regularly scheduled passenger service began between Minneapolis and Rochester twice a day.

As flight became more prevalent, Dr. Henry Plummer, the organizational genius at Mayo Clinic, implored Dr. Will Mayo to pursue opening a municipal airport quickly, before the city of Winona. Winona had a railway before Rochester, and air traffic to Rochester could be impacted if another city got the first government-endorsed facility in the region. Dr. Will agreed, and Rochester Airport Company, a division of Mayo Properties Association, was established. It purchased land east of Graham field, where Mayo High School and Meadow Park neighborhood exist today. The clinic made improvements over the years to ensure that patients were able to conveniently fly to Rochester. In 1945, Mayo Clinic gave the airport to the city, because as a privately owned company, Mayo was ineligible for government funding that became available after World War II. In 1960, the airport was moved to its current location on 2,400 acres of land. It became an international airport in 1995. In 2019, it served 359,000 passengers. Although the airport is owned by the city, Mayo continues to operate it.

In the 1950s, with the burgeoning of automobiles, buses, and airplanes, passenger train travel tapered off. The trains were being squeezed by the more economical fares that buses could offer and the speed and convenience that airplanes provided. The Chicago & North Western Railway, which was losing money, proposed ending passenger service. Communities on the line, including Rochester and Mayo Clinic, advocated for keeping the service. A quarter of the clinic's patients were still arriving by train in 1959. Eventually, on July 23, 1963, passenger train service to Rochester ended, ninety-nine years after it began.

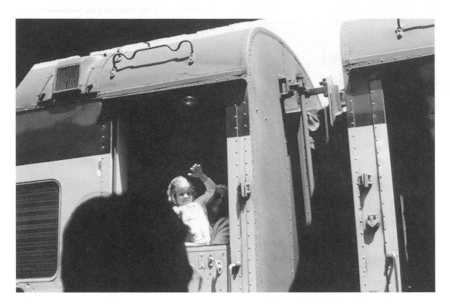

The author with her grandmother on the last passenger train out of Rochester, July 1963

My grandmother Pauline held me, a three-year-old, on the last train out of town, headed to Winona. Today, only the Canadian Pacific freight line comes through Rochester, carrying grains, coal, and freight containers on east-west tracks. The trains pass my grandparents' home, where I now live, several times in twenty-four hours. I notice it most in the evening. The grinding and squeaking of the wheels against the tracks crescendo as the train approaches, less than a mile away. The train whistle blows several times: long, long, short, short, long. This enduring mode of transportation has passed by this way for a century and a half, and those whistles remind me how much planning and perseverance, both altruistic and opportunistic, have built the city's connections to the rest of the world.

CHAPTER 3

Out of Destruction

Although the Zumbro River's floods repeatedly wreaked havoc through-out Rochester's first century and a quarter, the greatest devastation to the city occurred in 1883, when a massive tornado, referred to as a cyclone, swept through. Rochester had endured economic booms and busts from its inception in the 1850s through the early 1880s. As wheat crops and prices fluctuated, so did the well-being of the small community. Wheat rings organized by grain merchants and price gouging by the monopo-listic railroads persistently challenged the farmers and the businesses supporting them in town. Bad weather and repeated locust infestations damaged crops and the economy as well. But nothing threatened the existence of Rochester as much as the cyclone.

Ten years earlier, the first city directory described a vibrant town, offi-cially chartered and designated as the Olmsted County seat in 1858. The county was named after David Olmsted. Originally from Vermont, he had traded with the Ho-Chunk in Iowa and then at Long Prairie, Minne-sota; later he moved to St. Paul, where he founded a newspaper, became involved in territorial government, and was elected the city's first mayor. He never lived in the county that his friends in the legislature named for him, and he returned to Vermont, where he died in 1861.

Rochester's population was reported to be 1,424 in 1860, six years after George and Henrietta Head established it. By 1873, the popula-tion had tripled to 4,286. The city directory described the "chain of beautiful hills . . . the most enchanting panorama that could delight the vision," and the business listings cover several pages: "unsurpassed" hotels, three newspapers, three banks, seven dry goods stores, eighteen grocery stores, a men's clothing store, three jewelers, six harness shops, and one foundry were listed. Three women—Mrs. Ameigh, Mrs. Harris, Mrs. Stewart—had millinery shops on Broadway. Factories in town manufactured wagons, doors, sashes, plows, candy, shirts, soap, furniture, brooms, cigars, woolen clothing, and cheese. The grain elevator processed 700,000 bushels of wheat that year. Community and religious organizations were prevalent as well, including a large public school, eleven churches, a library, a chapter of the Grand Army of the Republic, a Union soldiers' veterans association, the Odd Fellows, the Young Men's Christian Association (YMCA), two temperance organizations, and a Masonic temple, chapter, and lodge. For the next decade, the city continued to grow as a booming business center fueled by the surrounding agriculture.

On the afternoon of Tuesday, August 21, 1883, dark clouds formed west of Rochester while residents went about their business unaware of the disaster that would strike that day and alter the city's destiny. A farmer working in his field that sultry summer day noticed the sky turn a coppery tint, and clouds began to shift in three different directions. As gusts of wind accelerated, dirt flew up and pelted him, causing him to run for cover. Two funnel clouds dropped from the sky and merged, and a massive, churning tornado headed into town along Cascade Creek. According to one of the Rochester newspapers, the suction of the cyclone pulled fish from the water and thrust them onto the banks. Hailstones described as being three inches in diameter, weighing a pound and a half, hurled out of the sky.

In town, at the Catholic Franciscan convent on Center Street, Mother Alfred Moes called all of the sisters inside when she saw the greenish-brown sky. They went into the basement, where they prayed fervently, hoping the convent would not topple over.

At the same time, Nina Cook, the eldest of nine girls, sat on her family's front porch with her grandmother and a few of her sisters. They watched the sky turn pale green and then copper. The next-oldest sister, Maggie, convinced the girls and their grandmother to go into the cellar. After the storm, they found their grandfather under the barn door, his teeth knocked out, but otherwise unharmed. Nina's mother was having tea at a neighbor's home a few blocks away. They, too, ran to the cellar and clung to each other while the entire house above them was blown off its foundation. As Mrs. Cook looked up, an injured horse flew overhead and a piece of glass struck her face, permanently blinding her in one eye. Next door to the Cooks' home, as one of their playmates ran toward a window to look out at the storm, a board crashed through the glass, impaling and killing her.

The relentless thunder, lightning, and high winds pounded until nightfall. After the storm subsided, citizens carrying kerosene lanterns combed through the debris, searching for survivors. Pinpoint lights bobbed through the darkness. Fires broke out sporadically. The injured were carried to homes, the convent, and a dance hall, where local physicians tended to them. One of the physicians, Dr. William Worrall Mayo, recruited Mother Alfred's congregation of sisters to assist in caring for the patients. Although the sisters were trained as teachers, he instructed them on how to care for the injured.

The following morning, relatives and friends lined up to file through the undertakers' parlors and furniture stores, where some of the deceased had been taken, looking for missing loved ones. Scores of hogs, sheep, cattle, and horses were killed. Featherless chickens wandered along Broadway. Trees stripped of their leaves and bark stood upright with bare, broken limbs, creating an apocalyptic scene.

The storm blazed a path of destruction thirty-five miles long and a mile wide. Subsequently, meteorologists categorized it as an F5 tornado. At least forty people died, twenty of them in Rochester, including John M. Cole, owner of one of the mills. The remains of a homeless man were found near the edge of town, and the storm pulled an infant out of its mother's arms. Train cars were scattered alongside the tracks, and the engineer was found crushed underneath an engine. A distraught young farmer hanged himself in a barn. One hundred fifty

Rochester after the 1883 cyclone. *HCOC*

families, more than five hundred people, were homeless, destitute, with only the clothes they were wearing when the storm hit. Two days later, teams of horses pulled wagons that had gathered at the Cook Hotel to carry ten of the deceased to Oakwood Cemetery for burial. An infant and five-year-old Nellie Irwin were among the dead. The *Rochester Post* reported the somber occasion: "No dirge was sung. No sound was heard but humble prayers and smothered moans of unutterable anguish. The only tributes left upon the close-clinging clay were silent, scalding tears."

As the community began recovering from the devastation, one person had a vision for the future that would change Rochester's path. Known for not letting a crisis go to waste, Mother Alfred Moes saw the need for a hospital that would care for the ill and injured in Rochester and the surrounding area.

Mother Alfred Moes,
founder of Saint Marys
Hospital. *WBFCHM*

She approached whom she judged to be the finest physician in town,
Dr. W. W. Mayo, who had established a medical practice in Rochester in
1864, shortly after he arrived as an examining surgeon for the Union
Army. He was reluctant to agree with her plan for a couple of reasons.
The small Rochester community had to replace and repair 150 homes
and many businesses, schools, and farms damaged by the cyclone. They
would be challenged to rebuild, let alone invest in a new expensive facility. Further, Dr. Mayo had worked as a pharmacist at Bellevue Hospital
in New York City. He found the conditions there deplorable, and at the
time, most people viewed hospitals as places to die, rather than heal.

But Mother Alfred had a reputation for overcoming barriers. Born with
the name Maria Catherine Moes, she, as well as her sister, Catherine,
immigrated to the United States from Remich, Luxembourg. As students
in a Catholic convent boarding school, they were inspired by the church's
call for priests and sisters to serve in the United States. Arriving in

November 1851, during one of the coldest winters on record, they traveled by stagecoach and steamboat from New York to Milwaukee. Trains only came as far west as Ohio in 1851. After they took their vows and joined a congregation in Notre Dame, Indiana, they began their vocations as teachers. Their congregation had a teaching mission, but when the Civil War erupted, under the mother superior's leadership, many sisters were retrained as nurses, and the congregation established eight hospitals and two hospital ships for the Union. Witnessing this transformation likely fueled Mother Alfred's aspiration to start a hospital in Rochester.

By then called Sister Alfred, she was frequently in conflicts with bishops because of her independent thinking. Eventually, in 1865, she convinced a priest to appoint her mother superior of a new congregation. In 1874, the Sisters of the Third Order of Saint Francis was incorporated in Joliet, Illinois. Mother Alfred and the sisters staffed twenty-three schools in six states, including Illinois, Ohio, Tennessee, Missouri, and Wisconsin. Discord within the congregation led Mother Alfred and twenty-four other women, including her sister, to found their own congregation. A bishop in Minnesota invited them to start a school in Rochester, where they opened the Academy of Our Lady of Lourdes in 1877 for students of all faiths. Initially a boarding school for girls, it also became a day school for boys and girls.

By the time the cyclone hit, six years later, the sisters had doubled their numbers within the congregation and opened schools in Minnesota, Ohio, and Kentucky.

Mother Alfred was persistent, and eventually Dr. W. W. Mayo agreed to staff a hospital—if she found a way to build one. He may have thought she would not be able to fund it. Four years later, in 1887, the congregation bought nine acres of land west of Rochester, and construction began a year later. The sisters had raised money by selling needlework, paintings, and wax flowers and giving music lessons. They were extraordinarily frugal, using flour sacks for pillows, chopping their own wood, and making their own soap. Their congregation had grown to managing twenty schools in several states. They accumulated the $40,000 they needed to build the hospital by pooling income from tuition and sales of property with funds some of the sisters inherited.

William Worrall Mayo had immigrated to the United States from Manchester, England, in 1845, at the age of twenty-six. His father died when he was seven; at fourteen, William became an apprentice in a tailor's shop, where he worked for the next seven years, attending evening classes taught by a Quaker tutor who inspired his love of the sciences. The Quakers educated women and men at a time when the Church of England taught only boys. Taking classes alongside female students may have contributed to William's appreciation for intelligent, capable women. One teacher, the well-known scientist John Dalton, especially inspired him with chemistry. Although he was interested in medicine, William continued the work he had known since a child: tailoring. Perhaps inspired by stories of opportunity in America that were prevalent at the time, William somewhat impulsively, as was his nature, boarded a ship bound for the United States. He made his way to Lafayette, Indiana, where he joined two tailors in business until 1849, when his fascination with science compelled him to begin medical school in La Porte, Indiana.

While in La Porte, William met Louise Wright, who had recently moved to Indiana. Louise, born in New York in 1825, moved west with an aunt and two uncles when she was seventeen, settling first in southeastern Michigan. She moved to La Porte, twenty miles away, with her uncles. In 1851, after William graduated, the couple married and lived in Lafayette. Dr. Mayo worked in a pharmacy. After they endured the loss of their baby boy Horace, Louise opened a millinery shop. She also took in boarders to supplement their income, supporting the family while William's medical practice grew. Soon they had a daughter, Gertrude Emily. Louise's millinery shop was successful enough that she moved it to a larger location and brought in a business partner. William spent the winter of 1853–54 at the University of Missouri Medical School in St. Louis, acquiring another medical degree. Louise and their daughter remained in Lafayette.

When William returned, he and a partner collaborated on research-ing urinalysis, newly recognized as having diagnostic potential. They saw patients, although not everyone could pay them adequately. Louise's income continued to be an important source of financial support for the family for many years.

Intrigued by news about the booming Minnesota Territory, William convinced Louise to move to St. Paul in 1855 so he could open a medical office. Louise opened the Fashionable Millinery, on Third Street, later called Kellogg Boulevard. However, William quickly determined that St. Paul had a surplus of doctors. Louise managed her shop and cared for their daughter while William spent time exploring the woods and lakes of northern Minnesota. Traveling by foot and birchbark canoe, he made part of his living testing copper samples along Lake Superior.

Frustrated with the politics of Minnesota's north woods and shore, William decided to return to practicing medicine. Despite the success of Louise's store, in 1856, the couple moved to a cabin owned by one of Louise's uncles within the Big Woods area on land near the Minnesota River from which the Dakota had recently been removed, a few miles from the growing town of Le Sueur. For the first time, the family was living in a cabin located far from any city or village.

Louise noted that their nearest "white neighbor" was fifteen miles away. Since she could no longer run her millinery business, she turned her attention to homesteading. Women living this remotely needed to make most everything by hand, including soap, candles, butter, and cheese. In her attempts to become self-sufficient, Louise was severely injured when she inhaled lye fumes as she tried to make soap in the cabin. This experience, plus the small size of their cabin, motivated her to begin spending as much time as possible outdoors, inspiring new interests and hobbies, including astronomy. "It was a rough, hard, country," Louise recalled. "A few folk were comfortable, but most had to struggle to keep body and soul together."

Realizing that this rural location would not work for a doctor's office due to the lack of patients, Louise and William purchased two lots in Le Sueur in late 1858. Before they moved into town, on March 11, 1859, Louise gave birth to Sarah Frances in their crowded cabin.

William turned his attention back to establishing a medical practice as the family settled into life in Le Sueur. Louise tended a garden that helped supply William with herbal medicines. She developed expertise in botany and the native plants used for healing: hyssop, tansy plant, yarrow, comfrey, and catnip. Trude, their oldest daughter, was school age, but the family endured another loss when her baby sister, Sarah Frances, died at eighteen months old. In the eight years of their marriage, Louise and William had lost two children and moved three times. In 1861, their son William James was born. They remained living in Le Sueur until after the US–Dakota War, when William was appointed by President Lincoln to examine Union Army recruits.

The Mayo family moved to Rochester in 1864, a few months after William had begun working there conducting examinations for the Union Army. They built a house two blocks from Broadway. Dr. Mayo opened his practice in a leased office over a drugstore, often traveling by horse and buggy to visit patients. As was the custom in places without a hospital, he often performed surgery in the patient's home, usually in the kitchen. There were several other physicians in town at the time, including women, some with medical degrees and some with extensive experience as midwives. Dr. Mayo had a formal education, and he traveled to keep up on the most recent practices. He and his wife mortgaged their home early in his practice to purchase a microscope to aid in his ability to diagnose.

Beyond Mother Alfred's tenacity in building a hospital, it is likely that Mayo Clinic being in Rochester in the middle of a prairie is due to Louise Wright Mayo putting her foot down and insisting the family would not move again after they arrived in Rochester. In addition to their frequent moves, Dr. Mayo had been away many times for extended periods to further his education and explore. Louise's insistence that the family stay put fostered stability for the family and eventually for Dr. Mayo's practice. One might argue that the world-renowned medical center could not have evolved if he had continued to relocate.

Dr. Mayo remained restless and attempted to move again. In the spring of 1873, doctors in St. Paul convinced him to shift his practice there to be closer to more colleagues of his caliber and to a medical school. Louise reaffirmed her commitment that the family, now larger with the birth of Charles Horace in 1865, would not move, so William commuted to the new practice while his family remained in Rochester. The venture lasted barely a year. The St. Paul practice was not prospering, and the commute was challenging and dangerous. William became stranded in Kasson, Minnesota, on his way home during a snowstorm in the winter of 1874. Impatient when the trains stopped running, he walked fifteen miles back to Rochester, through snow drifting up to eight feet deep along the railroad tracks. Soon after this incident, William relocated his practice to Rochester, this time for good.

Upon his return, Louise and William purchased a thirty-five-acre farm in 1875, just east of Rochester. They built a large house, including a tower for a telescope in support of Louise's interest in astronomy. She inspired her children with her love of the stars. Years later, as adults, her sons incorporated stargazing towers into their homes.

William continued to practice and teach his sons until they went to medical school. They frequently joined him on patient visits and even assisted in surgeries when they were still young—so young that Charlie had to stand on a box to be tall enough to help. Will graduated from University of Michigan Medical School and returned to Rochester in 1883. Charlie joined the practice in 1888 after graduating from Northwestern University.

As soon as Mother Alfred and the sisters had acquired the property for the hospital, Dr. Mayo and his sons, known as Dr. Will and Dr. Charlie, began designing it. They visited hospitals on the East Coast, learning as much as they could about the best possible construction techniques, floor plans, lighting, and management. Mother Alfred selected the contractor and oversaw the construction of the hospital, just as she had for many schools. She was often seen out among piles of bricks, poring over the plans as the work proceeded.

On September 30, 1889, the first patient was admitted to Saint Marys Hospital. Mother Alfred and six sisters staffed the twenty-seven-bed facility around the clock, providing all of the nursing, cooking, and cleaning.

Their days began well before dawn and ended near midnight. Because the sisters had been trained as teachers, not nurses, Mother Alfred chose the most dedicated, hardworking women in her congregation to open the facility.

The *Rochester Post* reported the opening of the three-story, four-thousand-square-foot red brick building. Among the innovations were maple floors with two thicknesses of felt underlayment, placed between the wood surface and the subflooring, to make them as quiet as possible. Wards of patients were placed on each floor. The first floor also held the reception parlor, offices, pantry, and kitchen. An eighty-gallon boiler in the kitchen heated water that was piped throughout the building. A bay window and skylight, built into the twelve-foot-square surgical suite on the second floor, ensured optimal light for operations. The chapel and sacristy were on the third floor, along with dormitory rooms for the

▲ *Saint Marys Hospital in 1889. Right: Architects' drawing of the hospital.*

dominant leader was not surprising. Except for Sister Barbara, she was twenty to thirty years older than the rest of the Sisters, and her judgment and executive ability always had been unquestioned.

But as might be expected, not everyone was comfortable with Mother Alfred's vigorous ways

Saint Marys Hospital, 1889. *WBFCHM*

sisters. The third floor was also home to a large recreation hall, allowing patients to exercise and access reading material during their stay.

The newspaper noted that the hospital was complete with the modern convenience of running hot and cold water, and gas lighting would be added soon. The patient rooms were large and well lighted and ventilated. Further, the article noted that "everything about the building is clean and new and every convenience has been provided to make the place pleasant and homelike for the sick."

Saint Marys was not the first hospital in Rochester. The Second Minnesota Hospital for the Insane had opened ten years earlier, with a capacity of seventy to eighty patients. Minnesota's first hospital for the mentally ill, built in St. Peter, had reached its limit of seven hundred patients. Rather than expand it, the legislature decided to start a second hospital in Rochester. Coincidentally, the same day that the *Rochester Post* reported the opening of Saint Marys, it also reported the results of an investigation of maltreatment and abuse of patients at the Hospital for the Insane in Rochester. Although Superintendent Dr. J. E. Bowers was absolved of wrongdoing, he chose to resign. He claimed that of the two thousand patients treated during his tenure, only ninety-six cases of concern were raised, and many of those were never brought to his attention because the attendants had a pact among themselves not to report wrongful acts. The governor's review committee made various recommendations about the hiring and supervision of attendants in the future. The publicity detailing poor treatment at a local hospital affirmed the relatively negative attitudes of the general public toward hospital care.

In addition to public wariness about hospitals, the sisters encountered religious discrimination. When Saint Marys opened, it accepted patients regardless of color, sex, financial status, or religion. Mother Alfred stated clearly, "The cause of suffering humanity knows no religion and no sex; the charity of the Sisters of St. Francis is as broad as their religion." Mother Alfred chose to affiliate with Dr. Mayo because she considered him the most competent physician in town. The fact he was an Episcopalian did not deter her, nor did it prevent him from committing to work with her.

Although Mother Alfred and Dr. Mayo could see beyond the borders of their faiths, many people and physicians in town could not. Anti-Catholicism had increased between 1860 and 1890, as the Catholic population in the United States tripled. In 1887, the American Protective Association, a predecessor to the Ku Klux Klan and the most vehement anti-Catholic movement in the nation, had organized in Clinton, Iowa, 250 miles from Rochester. According to Sister Ellen Whelan, a historian of the congregation, "Ardent Protestants would have none of an institution that was managed by black-robed nuns and in which there was a chapel set aside for the exercises of popery." Eventually the successful patient outcomes of the Mayo physicians and sisters overcame hesitancy in the community.

Mother Alfred was sixty-one years old when Saint Marys Hospital opened. With great forethought, she chose a successor who could lead the hospital during its next phase. She reassigned Sister Joseph Dempsey, who had been directress of one of the congregation's schools in Kentucky. Sister Joseph might have seemed like a curious choice because she had no experience as a nurse. In fact, none of the sisters did because the congregation had a teaching mission.

Fortunately, Dr. W. W. Mayo hired Edith Graham, a local woman who was trained as a nurse. After completing her education in the Olmsted County School system, Edith had taught in the area until she was twenty years old. In 1887, she, her sister Dinah, and two of their friends decided to go to nursing school at the Chicago Hospital for Women and Children, three hundred miles away. Undoubtedly, Edith's mother, Jane Twentyman Graham, had influenced them. Jane was "a woman of rare courage, deep religious faith, warm sympathy and a natural talent for soothing the sick and making them comfortable." She was also an accomplished midwife; her children estimated that throughout her career, she had aided in the births of 243 babies without losing a mother or an infant, a record equivalent to, if not better than, most physicians.

Going away to nursing school must have taken courage. Not only were the young women far from home; they were in the midst of a bustling metropolis. In contrast to their home in a prairie town of four thousand people, Chicago was one of the fastest-growing cities in the United States and the second-largest city behind New York. When Edith completed her nurse's training, the school assigned her to her first employer, a doctor in Chicago. Legend has it that when she reported for duty, he fired her on the spot, claiming she was "too young and too beautiful." Edith was twenty-two years old, was five feet two and a half inches tall, and had brown eyes and hair.

Edith returned to Rochester looking for work shortly after Saint Marys opened. Luckily, according to many who retell the story, Dr. Mayo "was not a man to allow a woman's beauty to obscure her professional qualifications." He originally hired her to administer anesthesia. Up until then, male interns administered the chloroform, but often they became so engaged in watching the operation that they neglected the patient. Dr. Mayo taught Edith to give the chloroform and monitor the patient's condition during surgeries.

Dr. Mayo was by now nearing the end of his career. He was seventy when the hospital opened—and yet the rest of his medical team was quite young: Dr. Will was twenty-seven, Dr. Charlie was twenty-three, and Edith was twenty-two. Dr. Mayo found himself spending quite a bit of time convincing patients that they were in good hands despite his colleagues' youthful looks.

Since surgery initially was conducted only a few mornings a week, Edith worked in the Mayos' office helping with patient visits. Occasionally, she had the opportunity to indulge her passion for swiftly riding horses when Dr. Mayo sent her to check on the status of a patient living in the country. She also utilized her education, as the only formally trained nurse in the practice, to teach the sisters assigned to Saint Marys Hospital.

In 1892, Sister Joseph began her appointment as administrator of Saint Marys and the religious leader for the sisters assigned there. In addition, Sister Joseph became Dr. Will's first assistant in surgery, a role

Drs. William James, William Worrall, and Charles Horace Mayo, about 1890.
WBFCHM

she would fulfill with the utmost skill despite not having previous medical training. By the end of 1893, after being open only three years, Saint Marys provided care to three thousand patients, now drawing patients from outside Rochester.

Dr. Will married Hattie Damon in 1893. Dr. Charlie married Edith Graham after they had become acquainted in the surgical suites at Saint Marys. After their marriage, Edith left her role as nurse and devoted herself to being an ambassador for the Mayo practice by hosting internationally known guests and dedicating herself to their family. The Mayos hired Alice Magaw—Edith's dear friend, the maid of honor at her wedding, and her fellow nursing student in Chicago—to replace her in administering anesthesia.

It was the beginning of a prolific and illustrious career for Alice that would set high standards for anesthesia administration internationally. Alice built on what Edith had started in the operating rooms at Saint Marys. A few months after she started in her new position, the Mayos

sent her to Chicago to study using the microscope for pathological specimens, and they acquired a Leitz microscope from Berlin with a magni-
fying power of 12,000 diameters for her use in reviewing specimens.
Sending staff to learn the latest technology and methods became important in continuously improving the practice.

Alice's anesthetizing work became recognized nationally. She adopted
the open drop method of slowly administering ether and chloroform that
the Mayos had recently learned from a physician who had studied the
protocol in Berlin. She noted in her lectures and articles the need for
careful monitoring of the patient's pulse, respiration, and skin color. By
1906, Alice had administered anesthesia for over 14,000 cases—more
than anyone in the world had previously documented—and without an
anesthesia-related death. Her leadership in the new field of anesthesia
was such that historian Helen Clapesattle noted, "Her work drew more
widespread attention than that of any other member of the Rochester
group apart from the Mayo Brothers themselves." Alice became known
nationally as the "mother of anesthesia."

The brothers were interested in surgery, so they expanded the private
practice beyond the family, inviting Dr. August Stinchfield, Dr. Christopher Graham (Edith's brother), Dr. Gertrude Booker, and others to join
them, especially to support the medical aspect of the practice. By 1900,
they moved into larger leased space on the first floor of the Masonic
Temple building.

Dr. Henry Plummer joined the practice in 1901, bringing both his
medical expertise and his organizational genius. He and a colleague,
Mabel Root, implemented a patient registration system and a compre-
hensive, integrated medical record that allowed all information on a
patient—laboratory results, surgical records, and physician notes—to be
kept together. Previously, physicians recorded all of their patient notes
in their own ledger books, and in the beginning, they often did their
own laboratory work. If a patient saw multiple doctors, the staff would
have to haul the physician's ledger from one doctor's office to another.
Having all the patient's information recorded in one record allowed for
a more holistic view of the patient as they received services. In addition,

when each physician kept their own ledger, there was no way for them to easily consider all gallbladder cases, for example, a practice that limited their ability to conduct reviews of cases in order to improve their care for patients. The integrated record that Dr. Plummer and Mabel Root implemented became a cornerstone of the Mayo group practice, allowing them to provide better care than they might have been able to provide as independent practitioners.

In 1906, Dr. Will became president of the American Medical Association, spurring more national attention. To continue to expand the practice's reputation, Dr. Will convinced Maud Mellish to move from Chicago to Rochester to become the clinic's librarian and editor. Maud was initially reluctant to relocate to the small prairie town of Rochester. Dr. Will prevailed, insistent that not only did the practice need to organize the library, it needed someone to edit medical articles to high standards, so doctors could get the news of their excellent medical outcomes more broadly known though publication in the finest medical journals.

Maud Mellish Wilson (she married Dr. Louis B. Wilson after moving to Rochester) was instrumental in improving the quality of the articles that Mayo physicians wrote. Further, she arranged for the publication of their articles in book form, *The Collected Papers of the Mayo Clinic*, and she started publication of a medical journal, *The Proceedings of the Staff Meetings of the Mayo Clinic*, known nearly a hundred years after its inception as *Mayo Clinic Proceedings*—now one of the premier medical journals. They hired several artists to illustrate articles, also setting national standards for medical illustration. Maud and her staff contributed to the clinic's early success by ensuring that its reputation was extended nationally and internationally through fine publications. With the hiring of Maud and several others in 1907, the practice grew to forty physicians and employees in their leased office.

Patient outcomes were excellent, the result of recruiting high-caliber physicians, nurses, and staff; collaborating with the Sisters of Saint Francis at Saint Marys; and organizing themselves as a team dedicated to the patient. Dr. Will publicly advocated for an integrated approach to patient care in his address to the Rush Medical College graduating class of 1910: "The best interest of the patient is the only interest to be considered, and in order that the sick may have the benefit of advancing knowledge, union of forces is necessary. . . . It has become necessary to develop medicine as a cooperative science; the clinician, the specialist, and the laboratory workers uniting for the good of the patient."

As the Mayo practice's reputation grew, the numbers of patients coming to Rochester for care increased. The Mayo team performed over 5,500 surgical procedures in 1907. This number doubled in six short years. By 1913, the practice saw 24,684 patients, and 10,873 of them had surgery. The growth required Sister Joseph to expand Saint Marys Hospital. Additions to the hospital occurred in 1894, 1898, 1903, and 1909, bringing the facility to 360 beds from twenty-seven beds when it opened.

In 1912, Dr. Will relented to Dr. Plummer's insistence that they needed a building of their own to see patients, replacing several leased office spaces in downtown Rochester. Dr. Plummer headed a building committee to do the planning for a new facility that would facilitate the efficient flow of patients and records. They collaborated with Frank Ellerbe, an architect in St. Paul with a rising reputation. On Friday, March 6, 1914, 1,600 people arrived for the opening reception and tour of the new Mayo Clinic in downtown Rochester. The four-and-a-half-story red brick structure stood on the site of the first home that Louise and William Worrall Mayo built fifty years before and where a more modern fourteen-floor facility, the Siebens Building, stands today. From five to nine PM, guests streamed into a lobby finished with fumed oak walls, cork floors, wicker furniture, and large palms. The room was designed to comfortably hold 350 patients plus the family and friends accompanying them. Colorful potted plants surrounded a large fountain in the center. Employees, including the heads of departments, greeted visitors as they made their way through the building. An orchestra played while women of the Visiting Nurses Committee of the Civic League served refreshments. The funds paid to them for hosting the event would support a community visiting nurse program.

The first Mayo Clinic Building, 1914. *WBFCHM*

The Mayo Clinic's waiting room, 1914. *WBFCHM*

Local newspapers lauded the new facility's appearance and functionality. One reported that the decorative effects, peaceful surroundings, and alluring appointments "are conducive to a forgetfulness of one's physical suffering, calling forth the higher instinct of love for the aesthetic and sublime, giving to the broken in spirit a new vision that dispels gloom and bids him who enters here not all hope to abandon." Another described the layout as one "which will produce the accomplishment of the greatest possible good in the smallest possible time . . . [so] that the work may be accomplished with the highest degree of harmony and precision." A medical journal article noted that beyond their commitment to diagnosing and treating patients, the men and women who made up Mayo Clinic also conducted scientific investigation and promoted educational activities that were instrumental to supporting the medical profession. This description articulates the commitment to patient care, research, and education that soon became the basis for the organization's operations and the three shields in the Mayo brand.

The new facility was the first building in the world built specifically for a private group practice of physicians, now consisting of generalists and specialists. Forty physicians and two hundred support staff were involved in the practice at the time of the opening. A light system on the exam room doors signaled the status of roomed patients. The building facilitated smooth transit of medical records. In addition to the patient care areas, the building included maintenance shops— where they made many of the specialized implements they needed, like surgical instruments and operating room tables—as well as stenographers' desks, patient records, and a greenhouse, where a skillful gardener grew flowers for the lobby and routing desks throughout the building.

By the opening of the Mayo Clinic building in 1914, the primary tenets of the practice that would underpin its continued success were in place: patient care provided by highly skilled, dedicated physicians and staff who were supported by efficient processes; a commitment to researching causes of illness and continuously improving treatments; and educational activities and programs that supported continued development of current staff through regular meetings focused on learning and pro-grams that ensured a high-quality future workforce. Most importantly, all aspects of the organization were dedicated to the mission: the needs of the patient must come first. Mayo Clinic became known as the first integrated group practice in the world.

The growth continued, abating slightly in 1918–19, during World War I, when Mayo Clinic and the University of Minnesota physicians, nurses, and staff collaborated to staff Unit 26, a base hospital deployed to Allerey, France. After the war, the increase in patients coming to Rochester con-tinued. In 1924, 23,628 patients were seen at Mayo Clinic, almost dou-ble the number that were seen ten years earlier, when the clinic building opened. The growth spurred Dr. Plummer to design a new, larger facility, again with Frank Ellerbe's firm. Standing next to the original 1914 build-ing, the facility—known later as the Plummer Building—incorporates the humanism of the Italian Renaissance with ornate exterior and mar-ble, carved wood, and brass, including two sixteen-foot decorative bronze entry doors, weighing four thousand pounds each. In preparation for the building, the Mayo practice put in a heating, lighting, and water plant to serve its structures and others in the booming downtown. When the new fifteen-story facility opened in 1928, it increased the Mayo prac-tice's capacity to service its patients, which had grown to 74,000 annu-ally. A twenty-three-bell carillon was installed in the elegant tower on top of the building. The Mayo practice is the only medical center in North America with a carillon, which has been expanded to fifty-six bells, allowing the carillonneur to cover a four-and-a-half-octave range with the 40,000-pound instrument. The carillon marks the quarter hours, and concerts can still be heard throughout the downtown. Dr. Plummer, in collaboration with the Ellerbe architects, created a building that effi-ciently and innovatively supported patient care.

The growing Mayo medical practice had increased the need for hos-pital beds and hotels. Saint Marys Hospital grew, but not fast enough. A pedestrian subway—a tunnel—was built to shelter patients, staff, and visitors from harsh weather, connecting the clinic buildings with

A postcard of the Mayo Clinic Building, 1928, now called the Plummer Building.
Author's collection

the downtown hotels and hospitals that were opening to help meet the demand.

Several downtown hotels were centered on the culture of hospitality that began with the tavern built by George and Henrietta Head. The impressive four-story, eighty-room Cook Hotel opened in 1871 to meet the needs of those coming to Rochester for business and the theater. As the Mayo practice increased, some of the downtown hotels were used for medical procedures and convalescence. The Cook Hotel provided rooms during a rash of tonsillectomies in the 1890s.

Not only did the clinic and hospitals need to be top-notch; the hotels did, too, to equal the quality of the health care being provided and to counter stereotypes people on the coasts might have about a medical center in the middle of wheat fields.

Local investors in Rochester collaborated to finance the needs. John Kahler, a hotelier known for his attention to detail and commitment to customer service, purchased the impressive Cook Hotel in 1896. Kahler first worked to meet the expanding needs by purchasing a large home and converting it into the first Kahler Hotel. To support further growth, Kahler hired Frank Ellerbe, who was involved in designing the Mayo Clinic, to build the Zumbro Hotel, a state of the art facility based on John Kahler's travels to and experiences of impressive hotels in Europe. The building, with terra cotta and Carthage marble, opened in 1911 with 122 beds and sixty-five baths.

Shortly after the Zumbro Hotel was completed, Ellerbe and Kahler began plans for another option: an economical but friendly, homelike hotel. But the urgent need for additional hospital beds in Rochester due to the rapid increase in Mayo patients changed their plans for the facility. It opened in 1915 as the Colonial Hospital, with operating rooms instead of hotel rooms. Other small, specialized hospitals emerged in downtown as well, including the Worrall, Stanley, and Curie Hospitals.

The Ellerbe-Kahler collaboration, in conjunction with local investors, some of them physicians and administrators at Mayo Clinic, began plans for a new Kahler Hospital, which opened in 1921 with 210 hospital beds,

The lobby of the Kahler Hotel, 1955. *Photo by Clarence Stearns, MNHS*

150 convalescent beds, and 220 hotel beds. Over time, the hospital bed need was accommodated by hospitals in town. The Kahler Grand Hotel, still in operation, was the premier lodging place in Rochester for many decades. In addition to the luxurious interior, a Venetian Gothic design adorns the exterior of the top two stories. The need for fine hotels continues in Rochester. Most recently, in 2019, Gus and Andy Chafoulias, a local father-son team, built a nineteen-floor, 264-room luxury Hilton Hotel. A longtime developer in town, Gus Chafoulias erected increasingly impressive hotel facilities in Rochester and advocated for the skyway system that began connecting downtown buildings, complementing the underground pedestrian subways that today are many miles long, allowing visitors and people working downtown to navigate between buildings protected from adverse weather, including Minnesota's winters. In total, there are nearly six thousand hotel rooms in Rochester

today, in addition to a Ronald McDonald House with seventy guest rooms catering to families with seriously ill children in town for treatment and other patient-focused rooming facilities.

Around the same time the Ellerbe firm was designing the Kahler Hotel, hospitals, clinic buildings, and schools, it was involved in many other projects that are still admired in Rochester: the gates to Oakwood Cemetery; the Chateau Theater, which at the time it opened resembled a fourteenth-century French chateau; the First Presbyterian Church; and the Mayo Civic Auditorium, completed in 1939, the year that both Dr. Will and Dr. Charlie Mayo died. The Ellerbe contributions in Rochester continued with the gray granite ten-story Mayo Clinic building completed in 1953, despite supply shortages caused by the Korean War. Ten stories were added in 1969. In 2001, Mayo's largest facility to date was completed by Ellerbe-Becket: the Gonda Building, named for benefactors Leslie and Susan Gonda. The facility opened in 2001 with twenty-one floors and 1.5 million square feet.

Beyond designing clinics and hotels, the Ellerbe firm was also involved in the construction of fine homes, many of them in a neighborhood that would be referred to as Pill Hill. In 1917, the firm completed a Jacobethan Tudor home for Dr. Will and Hattie Mayo on College Street, now Fourth Street Southwest, a southern border of Pill Hill. Hattie, who had a gift for design, knew that their home needed to accommodate the family and to be a place to meet with and entertain local and international guests. She created detailed plans and collaborated with the Ellerbe architects to design the home that became known as the Foundation House. In 1938, the Mayos gave the home to Mayo Clinic for ongoing use to support medical collaboration and education, which is how it is still used today.

Also in 1917, Dr. Henry and Daisy Plummer began building a home farther south of the hospital on a quarry ridge facing south. Although the Plummers commissioned Ellerbe & Associates to design their home, Dr. Plummer provided several mechanical innovations: central vacuum system, intercom, dumbwaiter, security system, electric and gas lighting,

Mayo (right) and Gonda (left) Buildings, Mayo Clinic, 2000. *HCOC*

and the first gas furnace in Rochester. The five-story, 11,000-square-foot home, completed in 1924, had forty-nine rooms, ten bathrooms, a ball-room, a pipe organ, and five fireplaces. Its sixty-five-acre grounds also contained a heated pool, a water tower, a greenhouse, and two caves.

Ellerbe also designed a more modest neighborhood. Dr. W. W. and Louise Mayo's homestead east of town was sold to Mayo Clinic and became known as the Homestead neighborhood. In contrast to the elegant Pill Hill neighborhood, Ellerbe designed economical Quonset houses in 1945 to help meet the housing shortage in Rochester after World War II. Many resident doctors and their families lived at the Mayo Homestead Addition in southeast Rochester. Eventually, many grow-ing families found them small and uncomfortable and moved to other neighborhoods, often closer to downtown.

During the same decades that Ellerbe was designing homes in Roches-ter, a local man, Harold Crawford, became a highly regarded architect. A graduate of Rochester High School, Crawford returned to Rochester

The Plummers also built cottages for their caretaker and gardener. My grandfather was their gardener for a period, and he lived with his wife and son in the gardener's cottage when my father was in elementary school. When I was a child, my grandfather took me to visit Mrs. Plummer, who was still living in the house in the 1960s. A uniformed maid answered the door, and a uniformed nurse was at her side when we visited upstairs. Standing with my grandfather, I last saw her in the hospital. Daisy Plummer was a gifted pianist, and she dedicated herself to nurturing and funding many civic and arts organizations. She gave her home to the city of Rochester to further support the arts. The home and grounds have been popular venues for weddings and receptions—including mine, in 1983.

The Plummer House, about 1920. *MNHS*

in 1916 after graduating from University of Illinois School of Architecture and Harvard University. He worked on several projects for ten months before entering the army in 1917 to serve during World War I. After he returned to Rochester in 1919, he developed an architectural practice, designing in styles ranging from Tudor Revival to contemporary modern. He also designed a wide range of venues: a large horse barn, homes, schools, light plants, churches, gas stations, a creamery, and stores. The Rochester Public Library, built in 1936, is among his most appreciated buildings in downtown Rochester; when the city library moved to larger quarters, it became the Mayo Medical School. He also designed the first modern grocery store in Rochester in 1936, the Piggly Wiggly, a grocery chain that, notably, allowed customers to select goods from shelves for themselves.

In addition to the vast investments that the Sisters of St. Francis made in Saint Marys Hospital since it opened in 1889, ultimately 1,200 beds, they undertook a major construction project to house themselves. Completed in 1955, the motherhouse, built high above the city streets, along the western portion of the bluff that became known as Indian Heights, is a 425,000-square-foot facility originally planned to accommodate one thousand sisters. At the time, eight hundred women were members of the congregation, which staffed forty-four grade and high schools in six states, a hospital for convalescents, a school of music, and a college. Then known as the Sisters of the Third Order Regular St. Francis, Congregation of Our Lady of Lourdes, the women were moving from the old motherhouse: the school built by Mother Alfred Moes in 1877 when the congregation first came to Rochester. The women had hoped to build a motherhouse for some time, a place where they could train new sisters and care for their elderly, but they had deferred their intentions for themselves in order to meet other construction needs for those they

Assisi Heights. *Sisters of St. Francis*

served in the hospital and schools. Assisi Heights was the first building the sisters undertook for themselves.

The motherhouse is covered with a Mankato stone exterior and topped with red Spanish tile. Marble pillars support the lobby's ceiling, and terrazzo floors and acoustic ceilings are installed throughout the building. The impressive Italian Romanesque architecture, reminiscent of the Basilica of St. Francis in Assisi, Italy, was designed by the architectural firm Maguolo and Quick of St. Louis under the leadership of Mother Mary Alcuin McCarthy. The sisters had purchased 138 acres, part of the Klein family farm, and the home and grounds of Dr. Louis B. Wilson and his wives Maud Mellish Wilson and, after her death, Grace McCormick Wilson. Also on the acreage was a vast apple orchard.

When it opened, the motherhouse included an infirmary, chapel, extensive kitchen, library, auditorium, large fireplaces, recreation rooms, music room, science laboratory, sewing room, crafts room, and solariums; it also provided sitting rooms for visitors, a parlor for meeting the bishop, and a magnificent chapel. The bell tower rang three times a day, beginning at 5:30 AM. The *Rochester Post Bulletin* noted that the cost "is a tremendous financing undertaking for a group of women, who as individuals own nothing. . . . They state they will pay for it out of their savings with small donations from friends." This vast investment, in addition to the multiple expansions of Saint Marys Hospital, demonstrated that the sisters were quite on par with the Mayos and local investors in building hotels, clinic buildings, and hospitals in town.

CHAPTER 4

Potter's Field

In May 1897, a Rochester newspaper reported the death of Charles Jackson, "a colored man who has been a man of all work about the city for several years. . . . He was a genial character and had many friends in the city." Jackson, a twenty-four-year-old man who had moved to Rochester from Chicago, died of tuberculosis at the county poor farm. He was buried in Potter's Field at Oakwood Cemetery in an unmarked grave. If it were not for a newspaper clipping about his death filed in the African

Potter's Field, Oakwood Cemetery, 2021. *Photo by Brendan Bush*

American folder at the History Center of Olmsted County, nothing would be known about him, which remains an important piece of a larger story about the lives of people who were laid to rest in the unmarked graves at Potter's Field.

Most people in Rochester do not know that this large section of the cemetery exists, and the stories of those buried there are invisible and forgotten. Instead, most people are aware that Oakwood Cemetery holds the bodies of the founders of the city and of Mayo Clinic, including George and Henrietta Head, the Mayo family, Dr. Henry and Daisy Plummer; veterans of wars since the Civil War and their families; Merton Eastlick—Boy Hero of the Indian Massacre; and Bernice Pennington, the first Miss Minnesota. In 1883, many of those who perished in the cyclone were buried at Oakwood.

Colonel George Healy gave Rochester the land for the cemetery in 1862. An engineer from New York, he had worked on the Erie Canal, then moved to Rochester in its early years. He applied his skills as an engineer to lay out the cemetery. Progressive in many ways, Colonel Healy ignited a controversy when he offered the library a donation that was conditional on the purchase of "books and reading matter of a liberal nature." He was also unconventional in his views on defining heads of household. Many people today still consider the father of a family to be the only head of the household. Colonel Healy believed that households have two heads, the man and the woman. He demonstrated his commitment to this concept with the creation of the Healy headstone in Oakwood Cemetery, which has two columnar spires, one that records his name and the facts of his life and another spire of equal size for his wife, Theodosia.

Oakwood Cemetery, originally seventy-six acres, was founded as a public, not church-affiliated, burying ground. Deceased who had been buried elsewhere in town prior to its opening were moved to the new location along the Zumbro River, just blocks from downtown. The grounds are deeply shaded by majestic oaks and pines that tower over granite headstones of all sizes and shapes, with names and dates chiseled into the stone, assuring remembrance for at least a century or two. From its

Healy Headstone, Oakwood Cemetery. *Photo by Brendan Bush*

My husband, father, paternal grandparents, and great-grandparents are buried at Oakwood Cemetery. When I visit my family's graves, I sometimes pass a spacious section near the back of the cemetery with few trees, open and flat in contrast to the density of trees elsewhere. But I never noticed it until I read Charles Jackson's obituary. I had no idea that the area holds the bodies of so many people. I have walked past the grassy void, never wondering what was missing, my eyes focused on the tall granite stones. Like many aspects of my hometown's history, this field demonstrates yet another way that the legacy of those with good fortune—including my own family—endures physically, in contrast to the absence of stories of others.

inception, Oakwood Cemetery has been available for Christian (both Protestant and Catholic) and Jewish burials. The board of directors was equally diverse—unusually diverse given the tension between Catholics and Protestants that almost prevented Saint Marys Hospital from admitting both denominations in 1889. Today, 20,000 people are buried at Oakwood. A bell tower with a carillon and a chapel with Gothic arches and stained glass windows adorn the grounds. In the winter of 1918, during the influenza epidemic, a record sixty-five bodies were kept in the chapel crypt until spring, when they could be buried.

When the Oakwood Cemetery Association was formed, the State of Minnesota required that a portion of cemetery land be set aside for those who could not afford their own burials. Initially, this section was referred to as Potter's Field. In 1927, the cemetery groundskeeper estimated that over a thousand people had been buried in the public section, but the cemetery ledgers now list only 453 names. The recorded burials begin in 1878 and end in 1955. Nearly half of those buried in Potter's Field are stillborn babies and very young infants. Other causes of death range from cancers and heart disease to suicide, train and farm accidents, and a few deaths by revolvers. The ledger also reveals that residents of Rochester succumbed to dysentery, diphtheria, cholera, influenza, typhoid, and consumption (tuberculosis).

Potter's fields are historically known as places outside of towns where broken, unwanted pieces of pottery were thrown. In the New Testament, after Judas Iscariot betrayed Jesus, he threw down the silver he had received in a temple before taking his own life. The priests decided they could not put blood money in the church's coffers. Instead, they bought a potter's field as a burial place for foreigners. The ground was pocked with trenches after the clay was harvested, making it undesirable; the red clay stained the soil, resembling blood. Yet some consider a potter's field, purchased through the death of Jesus, a place of hope and salvation for those discarded by society. The Potter's Field at Oakwood Cemetery is a spacious section toward the back with many oak trees. Along the northern border of the section, clippings and brush are piled against the chain-link fence, a short distance from my husband's grave.

The life stories of most of the people buried in Potter's Field disappeared around the time they died, but a few stories can be patched together. One infant listed on the cemetery ledger was murdered. In 1903, Marie Dalberg—age twenty-two and unwed—strangled her newborn girl with a shoestring "out of shame," according to the local newspaper. She was caught as she tried to hide the infant's body in a sack of straw.

Marie had immigrated from Norway to join her uncle, a wagon maker, and his family, who were living in Rochester. Marie was arraigned in county court on a murder charge but was allowed to stay with a couple until she was able to stand trial. According to a St. Paul newspaper, Marie was ill, "at the point of death," at the time of her arraignment. Rather mysteriously, a few businessmen in town testified, advocating for her removal to a home in Minneapolis, where she was transferred rather than stand trial.

A few months later, another article in the *Rochester Post and Record* newspaper reported on a letter the sheriff received from the Florence Crittenton home in Minneapolis. The matron of the facility reported that Marie was now a "happy, light hearted girl and is thoroughly converted. . . . She takes an active interest in mission-work . . . helps distribute food to the poor and in every way is proving herself a pure, earnest worker." Marie was being paid for her work, which allowed her to pay for her room and still manage to save some money. The letter also reported that she had the misfortune of severely crushing her hand in an accident, causing her great pain, which somewhat contradicts the report of her being happy and lighthearted. After that article, little is known about Marie. At some point, she left the home, married, had two more children, was possibly widowed, and returned to Norway.

Marie Dalberg's painful story reveals the plight of a young woman trying to start a life in the United States at the turn of the twentieth century—as millions did. Probably inspired by letters from family members doing well and hoping to leave economic hardships behind, Marie came to live with her uncle and his family. Presumably, unmarried and pregnant, she was ostracized, while the baby's father continued with his life unaffected. His name was not mentioned in any of the news stories about the baby's death. He worked in town as a barber, then at the state hospital as a nurse or aide, and then as an accountant. Notice of his marriage to another woman appears in the newspaper a short time later.

Few details are known about the people buried at Potter's Field, graves that go unmarked and unvisited year after year. What life was possible for the daughter of an unmarried woman in Rochester in 1903? Why was Charles Jackson, who appeared to be skilled, not fully employed by a business in town or a business owner himself? Why did he end up living at the poor farm? Was he barred from the sanatoriums, where the only known treatments for tuberculosis were available? And what about Ferdinand Gramse and the others who committed suicide? What was Alice Wise of London, England, doing in Rochester? The cemetery ledger lists name after name: Ole Ruenos, Betsy Evans, Jack Carrigan, Aver Larsen, Bertha Martin, John Hagan, Baby Girl Slawson. . . .

Potter's Field at Oakwood Cemetery is not the only location in Rochester with unmarked graves. Minnesota's Second Hospital for the Insane, established January 1, 1879, and renamed Rochester State Hospital in

1893, held 2,019 people buried on its grounds in carefully platted and recorded—but mostly unmarked—graves. The land is now part of the Quarry Hill Nature Center grounds. A group of local citizens led an effort to begin marking the graves in 2007. Before this cemetery was established, the state hospital had buried forty-one men and thirty-five women somewhere in Rosemont Cemetery. These seventy-six people are buried in unmarked graves in an unknown location.

Of the people buried at the state hospital, most surprising is William Henry Costley, the first male slave to be freed by Abraham Lincoln when he won a case he argued before the Illinois Supreme Court in 1841. William's mother, Nance Legins-Costley, was kept as an indentured servant—a device used by enslavers to hold people in bondage in a free state. Nance bravely began fighting for her freedom and human rights in 1827, when she was thirteen years old, arguing that she had not consented to indentured servitude. Lincoln won the case, and she and her two young daughters and ten-month-old son, William, were freed from indenture.

William was born and raised in Pekin, Illinois. In 1864, he joined the Twenty-Ninth Illinois Regiment of US Colored Troops, the only Black regiment from Illinois and the largest of all Illinois regiments. That unit was part of the Union Army when it entered Galveston, Texas, on June 19, 1865, two years after the end of the Civil War and the Emancipation Proclamation, to free Black people still illegally enslaved. The date, known as Juneteenth, is now a federal holiday. After serving in the Civil War, William joined one of the four "colored" army infantry units that became known as the Buffalo soldiers, which were deployed to various conflicts, including fighting Native Americans in the West.

William moved to Minneapolis in the 1880s. The specific reason for his hospitalization at the state hospital in Rochester is unknown. He died October 1, 1888, at age forty-eight; the cause of death was listed as general paresis, a neuropsychiatric disorder. He was buried in the hospital cemetery in an unmarked grave, along with many other patients, until the community began placing grave markers in 2007. His mother died in Peoria a few years after he did, and she was buried in a cemetery that was neglected and nearly forgotten until recently. In the 1930s, the city paved over the area without moving most of the graves. She lies somewhere underneath a commercial development containing an auto garage, union hall, and muffler shop.

The story of Nance Legins-Costley's persistence in gaining freedom for herself and her children, along with William's story of service in the Civil War and in Galveston, Texas, on June 19, are inspirational and worthy of being remembered and retold. Fortunately, the stories have survived despite the near erasure of their identities when they were buried. William Costley's grave at the state hospital, along with Marie Dalberg's and Charles Jackson's presence at Potter's Field in Oakwood Cemetery, provide another perspective on life in Rochester.

Rochester State Hospital reached a peak occupancy of 1,700 in 1955. In 1982, with the movement to more community-based care for the mentally ill, it was closed amid controversy. Adequate alternatives did not seem available for several hundred residents; yet, in a seemingly rushed,

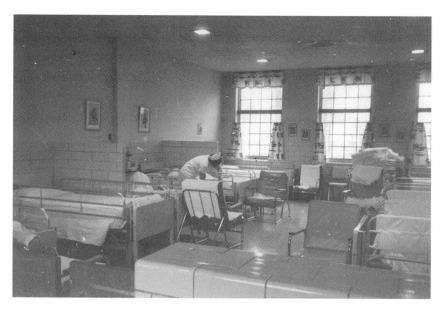

Rochester State Hospital, 1960s. *HCOC*

political, and financially motivated move, the state legislature closed the hospital and relocated those it deemed needing inpatient care to other state facilities, leaving some people without access to housing and care. In 1993, the Mayo Medical Center opened the Generose Building, a new psychiatric unit providing 130 beds to support their practice, which includes the local community.

Forty years later, reflecting on the decision to close the state hospital requires consideration of complex and competing priorities at the time. However, the impact of this decision, in the context of other funding changes, is that by 2016 Minnesota fell to last place in a ranking of states based on number of inpatient mental health beds, providing only 3.5 public beds per 100,000 people in the population. National policy guidelines recommend fifty beds per 100,000 people, which raises another issue of equity, not necessarily specific to Rochester, but clearly illuminating the inadequate resources statewide for caring for mental illness.

Over a couple of decades, the state hospital's 1,700 acres were divided among government uses. The City of Rochester had purchased 212 acres of its land in 1965 to create Quarry Hill Park, which evolved into a vibrant nature center where school classes, families, and visitors of all types come to learn and explore. The cemetery holding William Costley's grave is on the nature center's property. Olmsted County purchased two-thirds of the state hospital's land and built offices (including some for the county's public health department) and an innovative waste-to-energy facility. The latter opened in 1987, providing steam and electricity to over twenty-five buildings and reducing waste that was going to landfills by 90 percent. After some controversy, the remaining third was sold to the Federal Bureau of Prisons, which opened a seven-hundred-bed Federal Medical Center in 1984 for inmates requiring physical and mental care. The deep irony of a prison replacing a portion of the state hospital is difficult to ignore.

The unmarked graves in Oakwood Cemetery and at Quarry Hill illustrate how the legacies of people of color, mentally ill individuals, and economically poor people are all too often lost. The practice of burying people whose families do not have the resources to pay for a burial continues today. Olmsted County purchases lots at Oakwood Cemetery, now scattered through sections nineteen and twenty, not far from the section previously called Potter's Field. These graves are not marked with a headstone unless the family is able to pay for it. It seems both an injustice to them and a loss of historical knowledge, discarded stories of the Rochester community that could provide a more complete and accurate view about who we were then and who we are now.

CHAPTER 5

More Hidden Stories

Like the people interred in unmarked graves in Rochester, many stories remain buried. The legacies of people of color have not been collected in archives to the same extent that the lives of white people have, nor have they been included in the story of Rochester.

One excuse for not including African Americans in histories has been that few have lived in the area. The Black population in Rochester in 1920 was only thirty-seven people, 0.3 percent of the city's residents. By 1940, the number dropped to seventeen people out of the total city population of 26,312. According to the 1950 census, the Black population in Rochester was still only sixty-one, and it dropped again to forty-nine by the time of the 1960 US census, when the city had 40,663 residents. Subsequently, the Black population grew, and by 2019, 8.2 percent of Rochester's 118,935 residents were Black. But the *reasons* behind a missing story can be illuminating in themselves. Despite being a city of the North, and despite having provided soldiers and supplies for the Union Army to abolish slavery, Rochester has not been especially welcoming to people of color, which might account for the low population for over a century. This absence becomes an important thread of the city's past.

One of the first references to a Black person in the Rochester newspapers occurred in 1866 under the headline "The Everlasting N***** At School." The *Rochester City Post* reprinted an article (originally published in the *Winona Democrat* newspaper) describing an incident in a select private school in Rochester run by the Methodists. A twenty-year-old Black man attended school one day, causing parents of the other students to complain. They argued that his presence would interfere with their children's education; in effect, he would be a distraction. They said he could go to the public school if he wished an education. After consulting with the school's trustees, the principal reported that the Black student was "as good as anyone and would remain in the school as long as he behaved himself." The next day very few students attended.

In response, the editors of the Rochester paper noted that Democrats, the party of the South that had recently upheld slavery, seemed content to see "negros" only when they were in roles of servitude. The editor noted that should a Black person "enter an omnibus, church or school, in any other capacity than as a servant . . . he at once becomes excessively oppressive" in the eyes of some people; if Blacks were not admitted to schools, they would have to hire tutors, which would not be affordable. The article argues that it seemed "wrong, if not a positive crime to community . . . to compel anyone to grow up without an education. We have no sympathy with that fanatical sentimentality which extols the negro at the expense of the white race, but we are satisfied that unless an ignorant negro is a more desirable member of society than an ignorant white person, he should certainly be allowed and encouraged to obtain as good an education as he is capable of receiving."

Racial tensions clearly existed in Rochester in the 1860s, its formative years.

Not all of the discrimination was documented in the newspaper; much of it was likely far more subtle. Charles Jackson, the tradesmen and resident of the poor farm who died of tuberculosis in 1897 and was buried in Potter's Field, is likely an example of many African Americans in Rochester's early years who were employed as day laborers, and not by a business or other entity with more stability. Paralleling national trends, most Black people had jobs as laborers or household staff, or they started businesses of their own. In Rochester's early years, only a barbershop, a guesthouse, and a shoemaker were run by Black residents, despite the booming economy.

Rochester was not only a business hub in southeastern Minnesota; it was also known for its theater scene. Some of the entertainment was overtly racist. In the 1860s and '70s, opera houses premiered and regularly hosted the derogatory panoramas created by John Stevens depicting Dakota people as savages. In 1915, *The Birth of a Nation,* an extraordinarily racist film based on a novel titled *The Clansman,* was the first motion picture screened at the Metropolitan Theater in Rochester. Newspapers continued to note for thirty years, seemingly with pride, that *The Birth of a Nation* was premiered at the Metropolitan. In 1936, the Metropolitan was demolished to make way for a modern store, Montgomery Ward.

The white supremacist organization the Ku Klux Klan (KKK) was active in Rochester and particularly strong in membership during the 1920s. In September 1923, residents of Rochester found copies of the KKK's publication *Call of the Wild* on the doorstep of every home and business. The following day, two Rochester newspapers received threatening letters written in ink on white bedsheets. On March 3, 1924, people living on the north end of town reported hearing loud explosions and seeing a burning cross on a bluff. In 1925, a Klan spokesman gave an address at Rochester's Flag Day celebration, and the following year the Klan marched alongside their float in Rochester's July 4 parade. There has been great speculation about which city leaders may have been members, and it does not appear that there was any resistance to the organization. The overt presence of a group promoting white supremacy would certainly deter people of color from moving to Rochester, and it is not surprising that the number of Black citizens dropped between 1920 and 1940, although the city doubled in size during the same period, growing from 13,722 to 28,312 residents.

People of color were overtly discriminated against in various ways in the early decades of the 1900s. Saint Marys Hospital treated African American patients, but they were not allowed to use the main patient elevators or share a double hospital room with white patients. Black patients had to pay for a private room or wait until another Black patient needed a room. According to records kept by one of Mayo Clinic's first social workers, Juliet Eisendrath, Mayo Clinic required Black, Jewish,

KKK float in the parade on July 4, 1926, with the Metropolitan Theater in the background. *Courtesy Mike Pruett*

and Greek patients to provide a hundred-dollar deposit before they could receive care. In 2016, the Rochester newspaper published a woman's recollection of being a five-year-old who had just learned to read and seeing a sign that said "No Negros allowed" in the window of Lyman's Department Store in downtown Rochester.

Amid the racial tensions of these early years, it is surprising to know that in the fall of 1918, the captain of the Rochester High School football team was Black. William O'Shields, a talented fullback, was chosen to lead the football team in the 1918–19 school year, when they were state champion hopefuls after two strong preceding seasons. Unfortunately, that year's play was limited to one scrimmage, which they won against a team of medics in town—some with college football experience. The rest of the season was cancelled due to the influenza pandemic.

William O'Shields went on to the University of Minnesota, where he played on the football team and participated in track as a sprint runner. He graduated in 1932 with a degree in education and began teaching. In

William O'Shields, Rochester High School football captain, 1918. *From* The Crucible *(Rochester High School paper),* 1918, *clipping, HCOC*

CAPT. WM. O'SHIELDS
Who led what might have been a championship team.

1947, he became the first male health and physical education teacher at Cheyney State College in Pennsylvania, the nation's first historically Black college. He also coached football, track, cross-country, and basketball. In 2005, twenty-four years after his death, Cheyney University named their stadium O'Shields-Stevenson in honor of William O'Shields and another faculty member. That a Black student captained the football team in Rochester during the years that the Ku Klux Klan was active in town illuminates the complexity of influence in the community. But Rochester residents do not seem to know about William O'Shields and the stadium named for him.

Although the KKK seemed to decline in numbers and presence in Rochester by the end of the 1920s, there was a resurgence of overt racism in opposition to the nationwide civil rights movement of the 1960s. On August 22, 1963, six days before the Rev. Dr. Martin Luther King Jr. gave his famous "I Have a Dream" speech during the March on Washington, an Integration March was held in Rochester. Only thirty-eight of Rochester's 40,000 residents participated, walking down Broadway advocating for civil rights for all. During the parade, one bystander yelled, "You're headed the right direction!" as the parade made its way through town south from Silver Lake to Soldiers Field Park. At nine that evening, someone burned a cross in front of the Black-owned Avalon Hotel. In response, an article in the local paper stated in capital letters, "LET'S HAVE NO MORE CIVIL RIGHTS MARCHES IN ROCHESTER," claiming that such an event "just brings to the surface prejudice and hostile feelings that otherwise lie mostly dormant."

Other citizens wrote letters to the editor. A woman defended the status quo: "Rochester is known as a peaceful and friendly city all over the world, and people come from far and near to get well—not to a city fighting and disagreeing over nothing." She felt that the city officials who approved the permit for the march should be "ashamed of themselves," and if those who participated in the march did not like the way the city was run, "there are four roads leaving Rochester." Through the next week, other letters of criticism and support for the march followed. On August 29, the day after the March on Washington, under the headline, "Negro Demands Can't All Come 'Now!': But Handwriting on Wall," a *Post Bulletin* editorial acknowledged that the paper had originally printed concerns about the march taking place because of the potential for violence, but the editorial board had reconsidered, and they now added their "sincere congratulations to the leaders, marchers and spectators. It was a soul stirring event." The editors expressed support for civil rights, but not for immediate change and not for all the demands expressed in Washington, such as the two-dollar minimum wage. Instead, they argued that the focus should be on educational opportunity and voting rights: the "majority of Negros are not educated or trained to assume the roles they insist upon. . . . If Negros register

The civil rights march in Rochester, August 22, 1963. *Rochester Post Bulletin clipping, Rochester Public Library*

and vote in large numbers, many of their other demands will become reality without being forced down the throat of a reluctant citizenry."

Nearly sixty years later, in August 2021, another March on Washington took place, in reaction to the killing of George Floyd in Minneapolis in 2020. The call for voting rights was repeated, and this time the marchers demanded a fifteen-dollar-an-hour minimum wage. And that May, another march had been held in Rochester. This time hundreds of people, perhaps nearly a thousand, participated.

Through the twentieth century, people of color confronted obstacles in finding housing in Rochester. An exhibit at the History Center of Olmsted County in 2019 focused on the *Green Book*, a guide for Black travelers. The 1948 edition lists the few places available for Black visitors to stay in Rochester. Duke Ellington, Count Basie, heavyweight boxer Henry Armstrong, and many other well-known visitors to town, including those seeking care at Mayo Clinic, were denied hospitality at nearly every hotel.

The Avalon Hotel, listed in the *Green Book* guide, was initially built in 1919 by Samuel and Lena Sternberg. The Jewish couple moved to

Rochester in 1905 and opened a fast service lunch counter next to the Northwestern train depot, providing sandwiches and other quick food for passengers rushing through. Mr. Sternberg and several of their seven children were hired to translate Yiddish and assist Jewish patients at Mayo Clinic. Although the clinic's physicians were seeing a significant number of Jewish patients, there were only fourteen Jewish families living in Rochester. Lena Sternberg, soon known as Mama Sternberg, cooked kosher food for Orthodox Jews in the Sternberg home. When the need for Jewish accommodations outgrew the number of guests they and other Jewish families in town could host in their homes, the Sternbergs built the Northwestern Hotel at 301 North Broadway for Jewish visitors. The hotel could accommodate thirty guests in rooms that were equipped with hot water and steam heat. They served kosher food, and the hotel became a meeting place for visitors and local doctors, students, and intellectuals.

The Avalon Hotel, 1949. *HCOC*

In 1944, the Sternbergs sold the Northwestern Hotel to Verne and Mary Manning, who came to Rochester from Seattle, Washington, because of Mary's health. They opened the Avalon to Black guests because they themselves had been unable to find accommodations. Their first night in town, the Mannings had stayed in a park for several anxious hours until the Gatewood guesthouse made room for them. Shortly after the Avalon began operating, the need for housing for Black guests grew, and the Howard and Carolina Naves family converted their home into a boardinghouse and dining hall. In a city with more than thirty-nine hotels, the only places that welcomed Black travelers were the Samaritan Hotel, opened by the men's fellowship group of a church now known as Peace United Church of Christ; the Delux Motor Court; and the YWCA.

The inequity in housing for Black residents and visitors in Rochester was noted in the 1947 report compiled by Governor Luther W. Youngdahl's administration. In the publication, *The Negro and His Home in Minnesota,* the commission documented the housing conditions in Rochester. There were only six Black families living in town, and there were many Black visitors to Mayo Clinic who were denied accommodations despite a Minnesota statute that prohibited discrimination by hotels and restaurants. The report specifically mentioned that "The reputation of the state of Minnesota for fairness across the nation would be aided considerably if the hotels in Rochester would avoid any policies that were even suggestive of racial discrimination."

People of color who wished to own a home in Rochester were also subject to the discriminatory redlining practices linked to the Federal Housing Authority's loan programs. In many regions, lenders and real estate agents avoided selling or financing home purchases in neighborhoods that appeared in red on the maps created by the federal government's Home Owners' Loan Corporation (HOLC), a New Deal program that refinanced loans in default during the Depression. HOLC maps rated the credit risks of neighborhoods, assigning the highest risk to those where people of color lived predominantly. While recent evidence suggests that the maps were not directly used for redlining, they described neighborhoods in crude racial terms and gave the name to the practice.

But redlining was not the only discriminatory real estate practice implemented in Rochester; it is directly related to another specifically racist method of housing control. In 2021, Michael Resman, who owned a home in an affluent southwest neighborhood in Rochester for decades, discovered a discriminatory covenant in the deed to his house: "None of said respective tracts or any part thereof shall be sold to, used by or occupied by any person of Negro, Indian, Mongolian, Chinese or Japanese descent, provided however that restriction shall not apply to a bona fide servant employed by a resident thereon and housed in his residence." This property had been transferred in the 1930s from Mayo Clinic, and the covenant was included and signed by Dr. W. J. Mayo and Harry Harwick, the administer of the clinic. The property, undeveloped at the time, was near an area where the clinic was likely to grow in the future.

Other parts of town were affected as well. The land intended to become an Indian Heights housing development included restrictions that it only be used for residential purposes and not be sold or leased to anyone of "Negro or Mongolian descent." This meant that people of color were able to buy homes only in neighborhoods that did not have covenants. The Supreme Court ruled that the covenants were unenforceable in 1947. Yet the impact of the covenants and potentially the HOLC credit risk maps has been enduring. Rochester neighborhoods are still segregated, with more people of color disproportionately living in the southeast part of town, where the median value of homes on the market in 2021 was $249,900—the lowest of any town sector. The southwest sector, which includes the Pill Hill neighborhood, is less racially diverse and has the highest median property value of all of the sectors, $384,900, 35 percent higher than the southeast properties.

The local branch of the NAACP and the City of Rochester are actively engaged in a project to nullify the clauses, working with a statewide organization dedicated to helping property owners find and discharge the racist clauses. Those who were involved debated about whether the wording should be stricken entirely. Many advocated for leaving the covenants in the deeds, along with the wording of nullification, so that the evidence of the past discriminatory practices would be preserved—and could not be denied.

My husband and I bought our first home in 1983 on a street that adjoined Mayo Medical Center property. I was appalled when I saw the racially discriminatory covenant included in our deed, but I did not do anything about it. Knowing it was no longer enforceable seemed sufficient. Now I wish I had insisted on a notation legally attached to the deed that would have nullified the restriction, just so people reading the deed later knew that someone did not agree with the sanctions.

Disparities show in other aspects of housing. People who rent housing rather than purchase homes are more likely to be cost burdened. While Blacks, Indigenous people, and people of color represent 15 percent of Olmsted County's population, they own 9 percent of the homes; they also represent 44 percent of those affected by homelessness.

In the 1960s, a few Black families moved to Rochester and experienced both welcoming attitudes and discrimination. The City of Rochester formed the Rochester Committee for Equal Opportunities in Housing, and it held a workshop in June 1963 to preemptively help the community understand the Minnesota Fair Housing Law, which had gone into effect in January of that year. In 1965, Rodney Mendenhall became the first Black faculty member at Rochester State Junior College, now Rochester Community and Technical College. He was hired to teach engineering technology. Originally from South Carolina, he had graduate degrees in science and had served as an officer in the Korean War. When he visited an apartment rental office in Rochester to inquire about leasing an apartment for his family, the secretary told him they did not have any openings. When Rodney told a colleague at the college about the challenges finding housing, the white colleague returned to the rental office with Rodney and asked to see the owner, who then said, "sure," he could rent an apartment from them.

Rodney's wife, Virginia Gibson Mendenhall, had a master's degree in English education and believed she would go crazy sitting at home, so she pursued a teaching position, despite the fact that in the 1960s, most women, especially those with children, did not work outside the home.

When she contacted the human resources director at the public school system, he was open to hiring her. The director of human resources had the authority to hire teachers, but probably because Virginia was Black, he convened a small committee of white men, school principals and administrators he thought would support hiring a Black teacher. They made her feel welcome, and she was hired to be an English teacher and librarian at the junior high school. The Rochester newspaper noted that she was employed in an article titled "1st Negro School Teacher Is Hired for City System."

Virginia remembers that reactions among faculty at the school were mixed—and that she met as much resistance to her being a married woman working as she did to being Black. One man, the principal, asked who would care for her son when she was working, and a male instructor made repeated comments about the good money the couple must be making with two incomes. Because she was light skinned, many people in town and many students may not have known she was Black. She did not make a point of her race unless it was relevant. Sometimes when teaching a text that included racial issues, she would tell students she was Black. Often they seemed surprised, but not concerned. Once when someone suggested that she be more open about being Black, she asked, "What do you want me to do? Put a sign on my back?"

Because of Virginia's light skin tone, some people assumed she and Rodney were an interracial couple, which tended to subject them to more racism than being a Black couple. Even their young son wondered, "Why is Mother different?" He had not been aware of race before moving to Rochester. The differences between Black and white people became apparent to him in first grade, when he was called names he had not heard before.

There was not much of a Black community for support. The Mendenhalls were one of about six Black families living in Rochester in the 1960s. Virginia recalled that the YMCA was welcoming; several Black men in Rochester were members, and her son went to Y camp in the summer. Rodney was a member of the Y's Men, an interracial group that provided opportunities for community and supported fundraising for the Y, including operating a very popular lot for selling Christmas trees.

Another Black woman, Jackie Trotter, came to Rochester in 1965. She was one of the founding members of the NAACP and later became the first Black social worker at the Rochester Public Schools. In the 1990s, she developed the first prejudice-reduction curriculum for use in Rochester's and the surrounding area's schools.

An engineer, George Thompson, came with his family to Rochester in 1968, when he was recruited by IBM. A graduate of Washington University who had lived in St. Louis and Atlanta, he was surprised that he did not see another Black person in Rochester during his first two weeks in town. Shortly after he arrived, he and his small son went to a shopping center. As they were walking toward the stores, a car of kids in the parking lot called them monkeys. The incident was deeply disturbing, especially since he was with his young son. For some reason, the kids in the car "had learned they could call us these things. . . . A lot of really good things happen [in Rochester], but also things can happen that mess up your day, and you could get your day messed up every day in Rochester. I see a lot of good things, but [I also see] the hate."

In 1970, Thompson was picked up on May 25, 2020, by Rochester police after a shooting at a local restaurant and put in a lineup. George was well over six feet tall. Authorities determined the suspect was five foot seven, but there were so few Black men in town that police rounded up nearly all of them. When a white colleague at IBM told George that he and his family were welcome at his house if they ever felt unsafe, George was impressed that someone would be willing to endanger themselves and their family to protect his family.

That same year, George Thompson started a group, the Trendsetters, so Black members of the community had "someplace to go and be around people like ourselves." In addition to holding social events and supporting each other, they created annual calendars to celebrate Black culture. They also sold calendars to the school district, so others could learn. George became a community leader, engaging with the school district, University of Minnesota Rochester, the Rochester Police Department, the Diversity Council, and many other organizations to help members of the community understand and learn about each other. In addition to supporting community organizations, George has been a mentor to a countless number of young people of color, supporting their success in a community that remains very white. And his son, the little boy who endured being called a monkey by a car full of kids, went on to become a record-breaking running back with the University of Minnesota Gophers and to play five seasons with the Green Bay Packers.

The discrimination continued and made the newspapers in 1974, when another IBM employee, George Gibbs, was denied membership at the Elks Club in Rochester because he was Black. The Rochester Human Rights Commission, which was formed in 1966, investigated the discrimination, and the state liquor commissioner ordered the City of Rochester to revoke the Elks' liquor license. The license was reinstated when the club changed its discriminatory practice.

After George Floyd was murdered on May 25, 2020, by a police officer in Minneapolis, many Rochester residents responded by placing Black Lives Matter signs on their front lawns. On September 17, 2020, in an echo of the Ku Klux Klan's anonymous distribution of material in· the 1920s, residents across town who displayed these signs received unsigned letters in the mail claiming that anyone who supported the movement also supported violence against police, along with a threat: "I know your address, I know who you are, but I'm not going to let you know who I am." Recipients found the letters creepy, weird, and unsettling. Some of them worried "something more would come" of the letters, but the Rochester police stated that because no overt threat was made, the letters would not be investigated.

The Asian American presence in the Rochester area today is similar to the national census, about six percent of the population. Various US exclusion acts restricted immigration from Asia between 1875 and 1975, and relatively few Asian Americans lived anywhere but on the coasts through much of the twentieth century. But during World War II, the Saint Marys School of Nursing, under the direction of Sisters Domitilla DuRocher and Antonia Rostomily, welcomed Japanese American women. After the attack on Pearl Harbor, President Franklin Roosevelt ordered the internment of 110,000 legal residents from Japan and their children, known as Nisei, who were American citizens. People were allowed to leave the camps if they were admitted to schools or could arrange housing and jobs away from the West Coast.

Bringing Japanese American women to Rochester was a bold move. According to the US census, there were no people of Asian descent living in Rochester in 1940. The Saint Marys School of Nursing and the Kahler School of Nursing, both organizations in Rochester affiliated with Mayo Clinic, invited more than fifty Nisei women into their nursing programs, more than any other educational facility in the nation. Further, Saint Marys Hospital hired seven other Japanese American women, some who were already nurses and others as clerical and other workers.

Fumiye Yoshida
Tacoma ~ Washington

Grace Obata
Cleveland ~ Ohio

Cadet nurses Fumiye Yoshida and Grace Obata at Saint Marys Hospital, 1940s. *WBFCHM*

According to sisters working at Saint Marys Hospital at the time, the women were "outstanding in their scholastic accomplishment as well as skillful in their nursing care of patients." In addition, the sisters noted that their help was greatly needed because "the hospital was desperate for nurses." Although some patients were uneasy around the nurses—one patient asked a student if she knew how to read—overall they reported being treated with respect. Once again, the Franciscan sisters demonstrated that even a small number of people acting according to their conscience can make a remarkable difference.

In the 1970s, as the Asian American population increased in Rochester, spurred by the relocation of Vietnamese, Cambodian, and Laotian people, many Asian residents reported experiencing discrimination since their arrival, including discriminatory practices against potential tenants by landlords. In a 1985 survey conducted by the Rochester School District, 57 percent of Asian American students reported having experienced harassment. Some of these students had lived in California before moving to Rochester; they felt scrutinized by Rochester police, shop owners, and residents who watched what they bought in stores with critical eyes.

Somali and Sudanese refugees began relocating to Rochester in the 1990s after the outbreak of civil war in their homelands. Again, housing discrimination was an issue. Language barriers were also a problem in the schools, as was employment, although IBM and Pemstar—a new electronics manufacturing company formed by former IBMers who had lost jobs in cutbacks—reached out to employ these new residents.

Not all discrimination is based on race. In 1980, Gay/Lesbian Community Services was organized to provide support to the gay and lesbian people of southeastern Minnesota. It was the first LGBTQ organization in Minnesota. The Salvation Army offered space and some funding, and several local churches were supportive. One of its first initiatives was to provide a resource phone line staffed by volunteers. In its first year, it received 1,115 calls. In 1986, the *Rochester Post Bulletin* published an editorial titled "Time to Revise Society's Views on Homosexuality." While the article was supportive of the LGBTQ initiatives, the subsequent letters to the editor expressed intolerance. This thread of commentary may have been the first public discourse on topics related to the gay community.

In 1997, the Rochester paper published an article about a lesbian couple who had moved to the city in 1990 and were still feeling unwelcome. Fearing discrimination, gay and lesbian residents hesitated to go public. They were not welcome at most churches, and some restaurants refused them service. At the same time, the City of Rochester was working on an ordinance to protect gays and lesbians. In 1998, Rochester held its first Pridefest, which received corporate support from the DFL of Olmsted County, IBM, the Rochester Police Department, the Rochester Public Library, and several churches and community organizations. After a statewide referendum made marriage equality the law in 2013, more couples became public about their relationships, but still there were few places for social gatherings: no restaurants or bars catered to this community. Rochester has thus been considered less welcoming than the Twin Cities. In 2018, LGBTQIA+ residents formed Rochester Pride, which serves a more diverse community that is representative of Rochester's increasing racial diversity and international composition.

To appreciate the strengths and challenges of a community, its residents have to see it, read about it, know it. But the stories of many people and communities are unrecognized, and the stories are now even harder to come by. In cities throughout the country, local news in general is less available. This is true in Rochester, as well. The city's newspaper, owned by an out-of-state entity, has reduced local news coverage substantially, gleaning much of its content from police reports, business sales transactions, and the diligence of a very few writers. A new local online news source, Med City Beat, is trying to cover more broadly, but its small number of staff limits the amount it can publish. Local television stations focus on daily briefings rather than in-depth stories. Another news source, public radio, has only two local employees. All of this leaves Rochester with limited venues for sharing the stories of its increasing diversity. One wonders how the city will be able to create a sense of community and belonging decades into the future.

CHAPTER 6

Women Take the Lead

The first act of civic leadership performed in Rochester by a woman of European descent was Henrietta Head's ride on a horse down Broadway just after George, her husband, had cleared the way for the road using oxen in 1854. From that point on, women were integral in establishing and building the city, although most of their stories have gone unrecognized until recently. Even now, stories of people who had opportunities for education or came from families that were financially secure, if not affluent, and who were white are the most recorded.

Women physicians were practicing medicine in Rochester beginning in the early 1860s. Dr. William Worrall Mayo collaborated with several of them. Most impressed by the abilities of Dr. Harriet Preston, he recommended her for membership in the Minnesota State Medical Society in 1870. His action caused an uproar within the medical community. Dr. Mayo claimed that Dr. Preston was "a thoroughly competent and qualified practitioner," and he had "the highest opinion of her ability." Male physicians who opposed granting her membership claimed that out of respect for "female delicacy," they would not be able to discuss topics such as congenital malformation of a penis, which was on the agenda for the meeting where her membership was being considered. The Minnesota physicians ultimately deferred the question to the American Medical Association (AMA), which took nearly a decade to grant women, including Dr. Preston, membership.

Dr. Gertrude Booker Granger was the first woman invited to join the Mayo practice, the sixth physician and only the second doctor outside of the Mayo family to do so. Originally from the nearby town of Eyota, she completed nursing school in Minneapolis and then earned her medical degree at the University of Minnesota in 1897. She headed up the optometry department, and in 1912 she published an article reviewing 14,000 cases, including inherited retinitis pigmentosa, blurred vision due to syphilis, and blindness caused by chemical exposure. In 1914, she became deputy director of public health in Rochester under Dr. Charlie Mayo, who had become the public health officer in 1912. Together they tackled a garbage problem by developing a sixty-acre hog farm that recycled food waste, and they promoted pasteurization and inspection of milk production to reduce the high incidence of tuberculosis, which was a leading cause of death in the early 1900s.

In 1877, the same year that Mother Alfred—eventually the founder of Saint Marys Hospital—came to Rochester and established a school, Susan B. Anthony, the nationally known women's suffragist, gave a lecture in town. She was probably the guest of one of the library associations or civic groups in town. On December 25, she spoke at Heaney's Hall, one of the city's largest venues. Although, according to the newspaper, the weather "was lowery and threatening and the condition of the streets and highways simply horrible," there was a "good and highly appreciative audience." She argued that it was time to give "intelligent mothers and wives of the country" the right to vote, especially since the Fifteenth Amendment had awarded this right to emancipated slaves and Mexican immigrants seven years earlier. Thousands of petitions were flowing into Washington, DC, and Anthony was confident women's right to vote would be secured soon. It took forty-three years—the Nineteenth Amendment finally passed in 1920—and Anthony did not live long enough to vote.

The suffrage movement was well underway in Rochester by the time of Anthony's visit. In 1866, Sarah Burger Stearns moved to Rochester from Michigan to join her husband, Ozora P. Stearns, a member of the

Olmsted Tigers who served on the frontier against the Dakota and in the Civil War and also an attorney who became mayor of Rochester that year. In 1869, she organized the Rochester Woman Suffrage Association, the first suffrage group in the state. She was a regular contributor to the *Rochester Post*, which was owned by Joseph A. Leonard, a progressive Maryland-born Lincoln Republican. Stearns wrote about the daily adversities that women encountered and strongly advocated for women's suffrage. A month before Anthony came to Rochester, the following appeared in the *Post*: "There is no reason why women should not vote . . . on all questions. Women have the same interest in government as men, and should have the same facilities for voting on all questions that men have. [The Constitution] ought to be so amended as to allow them to vote whenever and wherever men do."

Sarah Burger Stearns.
HCOC

She and Mary J. Champlin Colburn of Hastings arranged for a hearing at the Minnesota State Legislature in February 1867. They were the first to propose an amendment to the state constitution that would permit women to vote. They were not successful, but their attempt motivated women across the state to increase their efforts by organizing clubs and circulating petitions. At times, their advocacy shunned support for Black suffrage, also in contention in the 1860s.

Stearns and her husband moved to Duluth in 1872, and she continued her relentless campaign. She founded the Minnesota Woman Suffrage Movement in 1881 and remained involved with the organization for decades. Stearns was another of countless women who fought for suffrage but died (in 1904) without seeing women granted the right to vote.

Amelia Witherstine. *HCOC*

Minnesota's male voters approved a constitutional amendment in 1875 that allowed women to vote for school officers and to be eligible to hold school board positions. It was many years before a woman in Rochester took advantage of this opportunity. Amelia Hatfield Witherstine began serving on the Rochester school board in 1911; she was chair of the board from 1914 to 1923. When she ran for office, the *Olmsted County Democrat* stated, "Mrs. Witherstine is a woman of much common sense; her mind is analytical and her judgement is good. Though progressive, she is not a faddist. She is well educated, a splendid homemaker, and a brilliant club-woman." The endorsement is quite favorable given the interesting criteria. She actively supported the suffrage movement, and her name appears in many newspaper articles noting her involvement.

Sixty years later, Amelia's grandson, Chuck Withers, became the editor of the Rochester newspaper, and ironically, in 1974, he resisted a request by the local chapters of the National Organization of Women (NOW) and the Business and Professional Women's (BPW) Foundation to identify people mentioned in the paper by their first and last name regardless of sex or marital status. The newspaper's policy was to identify married women by their husband's name—such as Mrs. John (Mary) Doe. The organizations presented the editor with petitions signed by 190 people. The women said they would phone back in one week. If the newspaper refused to make the change, they would file a complaint with the Rochester Human Rights Commission, or they would take legal action. Chuck Withers claimed that it was "inconceivable" to him that the paper could agree to print the name of every person mentioned exactly the way the person wanted it. Eventually, the paper changed its practice for identifying women.

In 1880, three years after Susan B. Anthony's speech in Rochester, thirteen-year-old Edith Graham wrote an essay entitled "Women's Rights" for a school assignment. She boldly claimed that "women have as good a right to vote as men. And if everything was as it should be they would vote. . . . The idea of women not knowing enough to hold office, where you see one smart man you see a dozen smart women." Edith, who later

Newspaper attention to people's preferred names continued for decades. My husband became a subject of an article in 1983, after we were married. We both hyphenated our names, and his new name began appearing in various publications at the high school where he was principal. After the editor attended a high school hockey game and noted Ralph's new last name in the program, he had a reporter call the high school to verify the change and subsequently write a short article under a headline about the first city official to hyphenate his name.

became the first formally educated nurse at Saint Marys Hospital, continued her advocacy in partnership with her husband, Dr. Charlie Mayo, and through the Rochester Civic League. Edith was also committed to the importance of motherhood and was named Mother of the Year in 1940 by the Golden Rule Foundation. She received the award from Sara Roosevelt, President Franklin Roosevelt's mother, at the Waldorf Astoria Hotel in New York City.

In 1899, the Olmsted County Equal Suffrage Association was formed as a result of a meeting held at Grace Universalist Church. At their meetings, the women read papers they had written on the topics of women's advancement and intellectual capacity to vote. Marion Sloan, one of the earliest members of the church, had come to Rochester with her family when she was ten years old, and she became a successful teacher when she was fifteen. She and another woman opened a millinery and dress shop when she was twenty-three. Their shop, above the Union Drug Store, was the sole agency for the Singer Sewing Machine. Eventually, she returned to teaching, and after retiring, she devoted much energy to the suffrage movement. She was the vice president of the Minnesota Woman Suffrage Association in 1905–06 and was on the executive board in 1907. In February 1920, when at long last women were granted the right to vote, Marion Sloan received special recognition from the National American Woman Suffrage Association for her intrepid service to their cause. That fall, at age seventy-four, she was able to cast her first vote.

Marion Sloan and Amelia Witherstine were among many of the suffragists who also supported the temperance movement. Although the movement might seem prudish today, alcoholism was a serious public health issue in Rochester, in Minnesota, and in the United States. The State Hospital in Rochester that opened in 1879 was originally designated for inebriates. Rochester's first business was Head's Tavern, and a number of saloons followed. Jost Brewery began production in the late 1850s, shortly after the town was founded. In the 1860s, it was bought out by an employee, Henry Schuster, and grew to become one of the city's largest businesses. By 1910, Schuster Brewery was five stories high and employed fifty people, similar to the number involved in the Mayo practice at the time. The facility produced and distributed 30,000 to 50,000 barrels of lager beer a year for Rochester and the surrounding region.

Marion Sloan. *HCOC*

Schuster Brewery also sold a million bottles of a tonic that was four percent alcohol, claiming, among other benefits, it gave "great strength to nursing mother and her baby." Even Saint Marys Hospital provided it to patients. The temperance movement in Rochester had good reason to advocate for prohibition, which was actualized through the Eighteenth Amendment in 1920 and remained in place until 1933.

In addition to promoting the suffrage and temperance movements, women contributed to the community through civil organizations that focused on the health and well-being of the community. Rochester Women's Club became the first women's civic organization in 1894. In 1896, one of the club's initial accomplishments was to establish the first public restroom for women and children in Minnesota. Downtown merchants funded the facility with monthly financial contributions. Rochester was an important business center for the region, especially for farm families who came to town to shop and transact business; women and children did not have a place to wait or freshen up.

The Rochester Women's Club also provided cooking lessons and a free kindergarten. It went on to address several public health issues,

Schuster Brewery. *HCOC*

including advocating for a visiting nurse for the community, hiring a health inspector and a school nurse, establishing a dental clinic for children, and advocating for a truant officer for the public schools and a woman police officer. The latter was made possible in April 1913, when the Minnesota Legislature passed a bill allowing female officers; Minneapolis already had one. The *Rochester Daily Post and Record* reported that although Mayor William Richardson "is not a believer in unrestricted Woman Suffrage he realizes that there [are] times when a woman's tact and intuition would be invaluable in the discharge of police duty," and he would not hesitate to appoint a woman police officer. Records are vague about what happened next, but apparently in response to the Women's Club's advocacy, a few women became officers for a short time. Their presence in public records is not clear.

The Women's Club also supported the election of the first women on the school board. Gertrude Mayo Berkman was one of the organizers, and Edith Graham Mayo was president of the club, which changed its name in 1910 to the Women's Civic League; the group remains active in Rochester.

Many other community organizations and chapters of national organizations were founded by women in Rochester: Red Cross, Diversity Council, Women's Shelter. The Young Women's Christian Association (YWCA) was organized in 1919 in Rochester and housed in various locations, including what had been the first home of Dr. Charlie and Edith Mayo, known as the Red House. They provided housing to women who moved to town for work at a time when it was improper for women to live alone. They also provided opportunities for lunches and teas. From 1920 to 1932, girls were able to camp nearby on property in Oronoco owned by the Plummer and Judd families. Unfortunately, the camp lodge burned due to a lightning strike. During the Depression of the 1930s, the YWCA helped to alleviate joblessness among women by supporting an employment service. City police reached out to the organization in 1940 for assistance in combating juvenile delinquency. The Women's Resource Center within the YWCA was one of the area's organizations assisting women experiencing domestic abuse.

In the 1960s, the YMCA and YWCA collaborated on a joint building adjoining Soldiers Memorial Field Park, which opened in 1965. Membership rose from two hundred in the 1940s to nearly three thousand in the 1980s. In 1986, the YWCA and YMCA merged and became the Rochester Area Family YMCA. In 2017, the Rochester YMCA became part of the YMCA in the Twin Cities, the YMCA of the North.

The YWCA started children's programs, and the preschool program Y-Tots was especially well known. The YWCA also partnered with University of Minnesota Rochester to provide a school-age child program during the COVID pandemic, allowing children of university employees to adjust to suddenly imposed distance learning during the lockdown while their parents tried to work at home.

While women's clubs were an important avenue for women to make contributions to the community, women were not permitted to join any of the men's civic organizations until the 1984 US Supreme Court ruling in *Roberts v. United States Jaycees*. When the Jaycees, then exclusively a men's club, began admitting women in Minnesota, the national organization attempted to bar them. The Minnesota Supreme Court ruled in favor of admitting women, but the national organization appealed to the US Supreme Court, which upheld the Minnesota decision by a vote of 7–0 (two justices did not take part in the consideration or decision of the case).

Although the Supreme Court forced men's civic organizations to allow women, the clubs were slow to see the membership of women rise. A

One of my first childhood memories was finger painting in a large home that housed the Y before the newer building was built. I took babysitting, swimming, and Spanish classes in the new building. My daughter went to Y summer camps as a child, and now my grandchildren are swimming at the Y and participating in some of the same summer programming. In 2022, the Y is planning to close its building in Rochester and move to a more decentralized model of programing, as many organizations adapt to new patterns of engagement.

Rochester Post Bulletin article in 1988 noted that only seventy-two women had joined the clubs in Rochester, which had a total of 1,011 members, and over half of the women were members of the Jaycees alone. Women members among the Kiwanis, Lions, Rotary, and Sertoma Clubs averaged only three percent in 1988.

One of the first women to join one of the previously exclusive men's clubs was Marilyn Stewart. Marilyn joined the Rotary Club soon after it began admitting women in 1989, and she became the first woman president in 1996. A successful businessperson, she was one of the top real estate agents, and then a broker and real estate agency owner. After raising her children and deciding to pursue a career in business, Marilyn chose real estate because it would be one place where women were paid the same as men. She had been a first-grade teacher and had become involved in many community organizations while her children were growing up. She was so involved, often in leadership roles, her daughter Nancy asked, "Mom, do you always have to be president? Can't you just bring cookies and sit in the back row?" As Marilyn became increasingly involved in the Rochester business sector, a man in town advised her husband, "You're going to have to rein in your wife." Jack felt otherwise, and was an ardent supporter of Marilyn's business and community contributions.

In 1985, Marilyn joined the Rochester Chamber of Commerce, and in 1990 she became president. This was an important period of development for Rochester. Government agencies, including the city and county, the school district, and major employers, had recently completed a flood control project and were ready to focus on new initiatives. They began developing a long-term strategic plan for the region. Marilyn was on the steering committee, which decided to focus on economic development, downtown redevelopment, higher education, housing affordability, and local government cooperation. The final report recommended a specific group focus on advocating for expanding higher education opportunities in Rochester, including a four-year college or university.

At the time, the city's institutions of higher education included a two-year community and technical college, established in 1909, and Mayo

Clinic's medical school, which opened in 1972. Mayo Clinic also had one of the largest physician residency programs in the country. Various groups had studied the question of a four-year college since the 1970s, but this local group's advocacy brought action. Governor Tim Pawlenty appointed a committee to assess the city's higher education needs. From 2005 to 2007, Marilyn chaired the governor's committee, which held myriad public hearings and recruited support from many business and government leaders in the community. The City of Rochester took the unprecedented action of allocating $14 million from sales tax revenues to provide seed money. Ultimately, the University of Minnesota agreed to open a campus in Rochester.

Once a campus was approved, there was a scurry to find a location. Utilizing Marilyn's real estate expertise and in consultation with others in the local higher education advocacy group, the university leased two floors of downtown retail space near Mayo Clinic. The university's new campus focused on health sciences and technology, with the community, Mayo Clinic, IBM, and the nearby Hormel Institute in Austin, Minnesota, as key partners. Ten years after opening, University of Minnesota Rochester supports nearly a thousand students in a downtown setting where nursing, occupational therapy, and a wide range of undergraduate studies are integrated into the health sciences and bioinformatics environment of Rochester. It is a good thing that Marilyn Stewart did not just bring cookies and sit in the back of the room.

Women's contributions in government began with Amelia Witherstine's election to the school board in 1911. But it wasn't until the 1970s, after the women's movement began to disrupt long-held perceptions limiting their civic engagement to volunteer roles in community organizations, that women began to hold office to any significant extent in Rochester. Carol Kamper won election to the Rochester City Council in 1971, and the next year Rosemary Ahmann won a seat on the Olmsted County Board of Commissioners. A year after Kamper was elected, when she announced she was pregnant and would continue to serve on the council, the *Rochester Post Bulletin* published a cartoon showing a high chair pushed up to the table in the city council's chambers. Thirty years later, in 2003, after a few more women served on the Rochester City Council, Sandra Means became the first Black city council member. She served for fourteen years.

After a long lapse, women returned to the school board when Karen Ricklefs became chair in 1973. In 1975, Nancy Brataas became the first woman elected to the Minnesota State Senate. Sheila Kiscaden was elected to the same body in 1992. Both were Independent Republicans. In 2002, after that party reverted its name to "Republican" and began to shift to more conservative stances on social issues, Kiscaden ran and was reelected as an Independent. She continued to caucus with the Republicans until 2004, when they rejected her and moved her desk and office furniture out into the hall at the Minnesota State Capitol. The same day, she was invited to join the Democratic caucus. She remained in state government for several more years and made a bid for lieutenant governor before becoming a county commissioner, a position she has held since 2012.

By the 1970s, women began serving on almost every city and county board and commission, including planning and zoning, parks and recreation, downtown development, housing, agriculture extension, and corrections, among many others. In 1989, for the first time ever, women chaired the three most influential governing bodies in the Rochester area: Jean Michaels, Olmsted County Board chair; Nancy Selby, president of the Rochester City Council; and Pamela Smoldt, Rochester School District (ISD #535) board chair. However, the office of mayor remained out of reach. Jesse Howard ran unsuccessfully in 1977, losing the election by only thirty-one votes. Women did not hold on to all of the leadership positions for very long; they were replaced by men (especially in the city council president position) for decades. In 2018, Kim Norton was the first woman to become mayor, and in 2021 the mayor, city council president, city administrator, county board chair, county administrator, and school board chair were all women, an unprecedented slate of women in government leadership roles. In 2022, a man became the county board chair, and both the city council and county board remain predominately white.

Women lead Rochester

For the first time, women will be at the helm of the three primary units of local government based in Rochester. They are, from left, Jean Michaels, chairwoman of the Olmsted County Board, Nancy Selby, Rochester City Council president, and Pamela Smoldt, who in July becomes chairwoman of the Rochester School Board.   Post-Bulletin Photo by Merle Dalen

The *Rochester Post Bulletin* noted the chairmanships held by women on June 9, 1989. *Rochester Public Library*

In 1983, Ancy Tone Morse became the first woman appointed Minnesota district judge outside of the Twin Cities and the first woman judge in Olmsted County. Inspired by her grandfather, an attorney in the Brainerd and International Falls areas, she graduated from the University of Minnesota Law School, where she and the other few women in the program had to share the dean's secretary's restroom because there were no facilities in the school for women. She graduated in 1959 and moved to Rochester with her husband, a student at Mayo Clinic's medical school. There were no female lawyers in Rochester when they arrived, and she wanted to be home with her children, so she began practicing law out of her home, working with clients mostly in the neighborhood. She often walked to their homes for appointments. In the 1970s, she joined a Rochester law firm, and her reputation as an excellent attorney grew. With the encouragement of another attorney, Sandy Keith—one of her sometime adversaries in the courtroom—she applied for an open position on the district court and was appointed by Governor Rudy Perpich. In addition to her judicial contributions, Ancy Morse was a leader in another important nonprofit in Rochester, the Girl Scouts.

Morse joined a lineage of prominent attorneys from Rochester, including Frank B. Kellogg, a self-taught lawyer, who after being city and county attorney in the 1870s and 1880s became a senator from Minnesota and led anti-monopoly cases at the request of Theodore Roosevelt. Kellogg later served as secretary of state under Presidents Calvin Coolidge and Herbert Hoover. He coauthored the Kellogg-Briand Pact, for which he was awarded the Nobel Peace Prize in 1929. Harry Blackmun, an attorney for Mayo Clinic in the 1950s, was appointed to the Supreme Court by Richard Nixon. He was expected to be a conservative justice, and initially he voted along those lines. Over time, he voted more liberally, and in 1973, Justice Blackmun authored the court's opinion on *Roe v. Wade*, the landmark decision protecting a woman's right to have an abortion without excessive government restriction.

The same arc of women's influence exists in the business sphere. There were a surprising number of women business owners in the early decades. Women owned shops and boardinghouses. Women ran the second-largest business in Rochester—Saint Marys Hospital—from the day it opened in 1889: Mother Alfred, Sister Joseph, Sister Domitilla, Sister Mary Brigh, and Sister Generose Gervais. In addition to leading a 1,200-bed hospital, Sister Generose was appointed to the board of First National Bank in Rochester, a large regional financial institution, and the board of the Federal Reserve Bank of Minneapolis. She was the first woman to hold both of these board positions.

The leadership of other primary employers, Mayo Clinic and IBM, remained in men's hands for a long time. Shirley Weis became Mayo Clinic's chief administrative officer in 2007, a position she held until her retirement in 2013. Although Weis was replaced by a man, Christina

Zorn was appointed to the CAO position in 2021. No woman has been the physician leader of Mayo Clinic, its chief executive officer.

One Rochester woman, Jane Belau, has made contributions in a wide range of venues. She spent the 1960s as a homemaker caring for her three children and developing her talents as a visual artist and pianist. She regularly played the piano at Mayo Clinic to entertain patients and employees, complementing the healing sciences of the medical staff until the pandemic limited gatherings.

Belau supported the civil rights movement in the 1960s, and she became a statewide advocate for persons with disabilities, serving on state and national boards and councils devoted to accessibility and the needs of handicapped people. She also proved to be successful in the business world in 1979, when she became vice president for government affairs at Control Data Corporation, a large technology firm in Bloomington, Minnesota. She held this position for over a decade. She also found time to collaborate with a local restaurant owner to organize the Community Food Response, which redirects food surplus from restaurants to those in need. She not only organized the new endeavor; she successfully advocated legislation necessary to enable and encourage businesses to participate.

Despite all of these contributions, Belau is probably best known for her weekly cable news program (now viewed on YouTube), *The Belau Report*, which she began in 1974 and still produces as an octogenarian, covering local, regional, and national issues. Over the years, she interviewed Governor Ronald Reagan of California, Senator Ted Kennedy, Senator Paul Wellstone, Vice President Walter Mondale, and nearly every Minnesota governor since she started the program. Her life of public service illustrates a considerable range.

In addition to making significant contributions in their homes, community organizations, business, and government, women provided the foundation for the arts in Rochester. Daisy Berkman Plummer, a gifted pianist, became a patron for the arts, especially music, in many ways, including organizing the ensemble that became the Rochester Symphony and Orchestra and giving the home that she and Dr. Henry Plummer designed and built to the city of Rochester to continue promoting the arts. Judy Onofrio, a mixed-media visual artist, developed a national reputation for her work and became the director of the Rochester Art Center in 1970; she started the Total Arts Day Camp program, which has provided children with rich art experiences for over fifty years.

Women are also a part of public safety in Rochester. After the mention of women police officers in the early 1900s, little is said about women in public safety roles until the 1970s, when women tried to become police officers. One of the most visible attempts was made by Joy Fogarty, who challenged the Rochester Police Department's veteran's age wavier for five years, which gave a significant advantage to men, from 1972 to 1977. The Minnesota Department of Human Rights sided with Fogarty, and the case went to the Minnesota Supreme Court, which agreed that the Rochester Police Department policy was discriminatory, but the remedy was to change the veteran's preference waiver, rather than hire women.

Finally, in 1991, Rochester announced the hiring of the first woman police officer since the early decades. Officer Elisa Umpierre came into the department knowing she would not be welcomed by everyone. In addition to her formal training and experience as a security guard at the Minneapolis–St. Paul International Airport, she said she learned to be tough growing up with three older brothers. Acknowledging that she might not be as physically strong as the men in the department, she anticipated that a woman on the force could offer a different resource, like having a calming effect in certain situations, including domestic violence. At the time of her hiring, Police Chief Pat Farrell said, "We are finally getting into the modern world. It's long overdue."

Twenty-six years later, in 2017, the city paid out a $1 million settlement to former Lieutenant Umpierre in response to her complaint of racial bias within the police department. She had been terminated for making Facebook posts that stated her concerns about the department's use of excessive force and offered support for the Dakota pipeline protestors. At the time, Police Chief Roger Peterson noted, "When the expression of personal opinions impairs the ability of an individual to effectively perform their job and/or undermines the mission of the police department, we are obligated to address those issues." The previous year, the same chief had supported a white male officer who posted racially offensive posts on Facebook. "I know many people believe [he] should be terminated as a result of this incident," Peterson wrote at the time. "I don't, however, believe it would be the right thing to do." The male officer was suspended for ten days without pay.

In 2021, under a new police chief, there are fifteen women (11 percent) and fourteen officers of color (10 percent) among the 137 Rochester police officers. While this is possibly the most diverse the force has been, it is considerably below the gender and racial makeup of the community.

While the stories of women in leadership in a wide range of fields is inspiring, it is interesting to note that from Henrietta Head's ride down Broadway to form the first street in Rochester in 1854 to the successful passage of the Nineteenth Amendment in 1920, women were clearly visible. It is understandable that during the 1930s, there were fewer opportunities for men and women. After World War II, women were limited more than ever to being homemakers, nurses, and teachers— traditional spheres. It was not until the 1960s that the civil rights and women's rights movements forged new paths and opportunities for women, but still most opportunities were available only to women who had been educated and, in some cases, were married to men who were physicians at Mayo Clinic or in other influential positions in Rochester. In the future, it is imperative that all histories include the stories of all sectors of a community.

CHAPTER 7

Big Blue Comes to Town

The announcement of the most significant new business development in Rochester since the opening of Saint Marys Hospital in 1889 and the first Mayo Clinic buildings in 1914 and 1928 came in February 1956, when International Business Machines (IBM) announced it would "erect a huge plant . . . [with] 1,500 to be employed" by 1958. The corporation had purchased a 397-acre site northwest of downtown and planned to build facilities totaling 400,000 square feet. It would be the company's sixth major plant in the United States.

IBM chose Rochester after conducting a survey of eighty cities in the Midwest with populations of 25,000 to 75,000 and an adequate workforce, including skilled workers. In addition, IBM noted Rochester's excellent schools, recreational facilities, "the high degree of public interest in civic affairs, and [that] the city is devoid of slum areas and has no social, racial or religious tensions." Rochester was an extraordinarily homogenous community—and ironically, IBM would change that to some extent.

In addition to IBM's analysis of possible sites and encouragement from a local development company, Rochester Industrial Opportunities, Inc., the president of IBM, Thomas J. Watson, had a personal reason to approve the decision. Watson, an Army Air Corps bomber pilot, flew during World War II with Colonel Leland Fiegel, a Rochester man who died in an air crash in 1948. Watson maintained a relationship with Fiegel's family after the war, and he acknowledged that he was "delighted" Rochester had been chosen.

IBM's new buildings in Rochester, 1957–58. *HCOC*

With IBM precision, the plant was built and the employees were hired on schedule. The 576,000-square-foot facility—larger than initially planned—was more than half the size of the Pentagon. Eero Saarinen, who also designed Dulles Airport in Washington, DC, and the Gateway Arch in St. Louis, was the architect. The building's exterior was clad in blue glass. Five thousand people came to the grand opening on September 30, 1958, which was attended by Governor Orville Freeman; music was provided by the Minnesota Orchestra. By the time of the opening, IBM had already been in business in Rochester for two years. The company did not wait for the plant to be built. Shortly after the announcement in February 1956, IBM began leasing space in a former grocery store downtown that allowed the first Rochester product, the electro-mechanical 077 Numeric Collator, to roll off the assembly line in August 1956, two years before the new plant opened.

IBM's Type 077 Collator, manufactured in Rochester, 1956. *HCOC*

The Rochester IBM plant composition was innovative; it was both a research and development facility and a manufacturing plant. For the next several years, the Rochester IBM plant produced a variety of collators, card reader punch machines, teller terminals, and optical mark scoring machines. In 1964, the first 1060 data communication system was shipped, and the following year, IBM's new card reader and card punch, the 2540, which was used with the new System/360, was designed and produced in Rochester. The company transitioned to optical readers built for the US Postal Service, and they produced retail ticket encoders and checkout scanners for supermarkets. In 1969, IBM's first small computer, the System/3, was totally developed in Rochester, followed by the System/34, System/36, and System/38, a series of smaller computers offering advanced technology for small and medium-size businesses.

The facility added professional-level jobs like engineering and front-line manufacturing. The company projected that 70 percent of its workforce would be men, resulting in limited competition for employees in Rochester, since 80 percent of Mayo Clinic's and the hospital's workforces consisted of nurses, secretaries, and housekeepers—occupations typically held by women. Men made up the vast majority of the physicians, scientists, and administrators at the medical facilities. IBM hired and transferred engineers, business professionals, and line manufacturing workers from other plants.

While there was some competition for skilled labor in Rochester, IBM and Mayo Clinic collaborated on cardiac postoperative bedside monitoring instrumentation that went into use at Saint Marys Hospital in Rochester in 1973. The collaborative projects superseded hiring tensions between the two major employers in town. While it was never publicly stated, both entities sought good employee relationships to avoid unions, and amazingly, there are very few employees represented by unions in 2021.

During the 1960s, when IBM was growing quickly, it hired from the local area as well as regionally and nationally. But the hiring of people of color into the homogenous city caused some controversy. In September 1963, the Rochester newspaper published an article with the headline "IBM Dispels Rumors Concerning All-Out Drive to Employ Negroes: One Hired Last Month." A recruitment specialist from the Rochester IBM facility "quashed" rumors that the plant planned to recruit "eighteen to one hundred Negro employees." He confirmed that IBM had hired a Black person within the past month, but "dispelled widely circulated rumors that his company had an all-out drive to hire Negros." He explained that IBM was always looking for qualified employees. IBM had agreed to support President John F. Kennedy's "plans for progress," and the company would continue to hire employees who met the "qualifications and needs, regardless of race, creed, color or national origin." (Gender had not yet been added to the list.) The representative noted that the recent hire was a graduate of the University of Minnesota and a veteran who served in the US Navy for twenty-four years.

The IBM representative shared these clarifications at a luncheon meeting of the Rochester Committee for Equal Housing Opportunity, which was made up of several churches, the League of Women Voters, and the Governor's Human Rights Commission. There were only twenty people at the luncheon; however, it was the largest turnout the group had ever had.

The employee, George Gibbs, and Joyce, his wife, were in the process of moving to Rochester with their two children. "The employee" was quoted, although not identified, in the article. He said he did not feel he had been "subjected to any discrimination since his arrival in Rochester"; he "is said to have encountered no person who refused to let him look at potential homes for himself and family." Although the Gibbs family may not have experienced challenges in finding housing, they encountered

George Gibbs, IBM, 1970s. *Leilani Raashida Henry, Gibbs family*

other forms of bias over the years. In 1974, George was refused membership in the Elks Club—until the City of Rochester threatened to revoke
its liquor license. Already a member of a church, Joyce was asked if she
was going to join a Black church when it opened. She had always been
a Methodist, so she did not understand why people thought she would
change churches. Still today, it is not uncommon for people at Joyce's
retirement home to assume she is employed there, not a resident.

My father was employed at IBM in personnel, now known as human
resources, beginning in 1958. Everything at IBM seemed to be top secret.
He did not talk about his work much. When we were children, he told us
only that he "shuffled papers" at work. He worked long hours and carried
a heavy Samsonite briefcase to and from the plant, stuffed with those
papers. He often left in the morning before we were awake and sometimes came home late after we were in bed. He put pennies from his
pocket change out on his dresser for us to find in the morning and fill our
piggy banks. Another of my childhood memories is the large Christmas
program IBM held in the civic center, providing a Santa, treats, and gifts.

My father's start time was an odd number of minutes before 8 AM, not
like most businesses that begin exactly on the hour. With IBM precision,
employee start times in the morning were staggered every six minutes to
avoid congestion at the parking lot gates: 7:42 AM, 7:48 AM, and 7:54 AM,
for example, and corresponding end times. This staggered schedule also
helped reduce lines in the cafeteria. The first, second, and third shifts
were given forty-two, twenty-four, and eighteen minutes, respectively, for
their lunch breaks. The third shift certainly needed to be quick about eat-
ing. IBM also had a strict dress code until the 1990s. From the opening,
men working in offices wore white dress shirts and dark ties, suits, and
wing-tipped shoes. Women wore dresses—never pants or slacks. While
some people resented the uniformity, one former IBM employee noted
that there were many personal touches as well. She recalled receiving a
note from the plant manager when each of her children was born and a
silver spoon to commemorate the event.

After twenty years, in 1976, IBM had grown to 1.9 million square feet of space, over five hundred acres of land, and five thousand employees. They produced over fifty different products. When IBM could not build fast enough to support its own growth, the corporation leased space in places such as the Franciscan Sisters' convent and over a drugstore. Some of the buildings they occupied are now grocery stores and a training center for a nonprofit. In 1986, IBM celebrated its thirtieth anniversary in Rochester with seven thousand employees, and the plant had become the largest IBM facility under one contiguous roof. The facility covered 586 acres with thirty-five buildings.

In the late 1980s, the Application System/400, a midrange computer for small and medium-size businesses, was designed and produced at the Rochester plant. The AS/400 represented a new horizontal microcode and innovative attributes that signaled the beginning of a new generation of computers. The design included forty-eight times the storage capacity and ten times the processing speed. In the first full year of production, 12,000 AS/400s rolled off the assembly line in Rochester for distribution across North America and countries abroad, including Japan. IBM was tight-lipped about the impact on the local economy, but industry analysts estimated that the company added more than eight hundred employees to bring the plant to 7,800 employees, ensuring production around the clock.

The Rochester plant operated at high levels of efficiency and quality in both its design and production functions. In 1990, the plant was the recipient of a Malcolm Baldrige National Quality Award, the highest award for performance excellence in the United States. Out of 180,000 applicants, the Rochester IBM plant was one of four companies receiving the award in 1990 from President George H. W. Bush. The president noted during the awards ceremony that the Rochester facility spent five times the national average on employee education and training. He emphasized the importance of the United States remaining competitive in the international market and continuing to increase exports.

Despite the design and production success, challenges in the national and international markets began to impact the Rochester plant. During

the 1970s, the plant had become a major force in the design and production of disk drives and data storage products. The hard disk products were precedent-setting, with storage capacities from twenty to four
hundred megabytes. Although the data storage team continued to design
and produce high-quality products, the global market became increasingly competitive. In the 1990s, IBM reorganized the product line, and
disk drive manufacturing was centralized in Singapore. Ultimately, IBM
sold the disk drive business to Hitachi.

The sale of the disk drive line of business signaled the beginning
of sustained downsizing at the Rochester plant, which had reached a
peak of 8,100 employees in 1990–91. Five hundred positions were cut
in 1992, followed by the reduction of 1,900 positions in 1994. Seven
hundred of the positions were in manufacturing; portions of the workload were transferred to other plants in California, Japan, and Germany.
About 1,200 of the eliminated positions were temporary workers brought
on to meet workload demands. Employees were provided with an early
retirement option, retraining, and severance pay. By 1996, the plant was
down to 4,600 employees. Decreases continued for the next decade. In
2018, IBM sold its five-hundred-acre campus and thirty-four buildings
to a Los Angeles developer for $34 million, retaining a twelve-year lease
to occupy eight buildings.

By 2020, with an estimated 2,800 people employed at the plant, IBM's
new CEO, Arvind Krishna, announced that the technology giant would
be split in two in 2021, spinning off its application and infrastructure
divisions in a new public company and retaining a focus on hybrid cloud
services and artificial intelligence (AI). Employees in Rochester worked
in both of these arenas, so it is unknown who will remain working in
Rochester, especially when the twelve-year lease ends in 2030.

During its sixty-five years of activity, IBM had a sustained impact on
housing, neighborhoods, and schools in Rochester. In addition to providing jobs, the large expansion on the northwest side of town when
IBM arrived in the late 1950s resulted in the development and proliferation of suburbs. In many ways, Mayo Clinic and IBM existed in Rochester

in quite separate spheres. Their employees lived and worked in different parts of town, and IBM's research focus kept many of its initiatives secret. The plant was surrounded by fencing, and a security guard was posted at the entrance. Not much socializing occurred between the two corporate worlds, other than the specific projects they collaborated on. And neighborhoods developed nearby to support the IBM plant.

The emergence of neighborhoods in the northwest part of Rochester, in proximity to IBM, made the presence of neighborhoods throughout the city more obvious. In the first fifty years of life in the city, the 1850s through the early 1900s, only Upper Town and Lower Town existed. Rochester evolved into two sections as competing investors from Boston built a mill and attempted to develop a second downtown. Although the area was north of the founding businesses and homes of Rochester, it was referred to as Lower Town because it was downstream: the south branch of the Zumbro River flows north through the town. The two downtowns were intense rivals until 1883, when the tornado hit Lower Town harder than Upper Town. The core of downtown most evident today exists in what used to be called Upper Town.

Other neighborhoods emerged around Saint Marys Hospital. In the late 1880s, August and Bertha Kutzky moved to Rochester from a farm in Farmington Township, north of town. They bought ninety acres just north of the new hospital. August became an agent for Davis Sewing Machine Company, and as Rochester grew, he also became a developer, selling lots on an installment basis. The Kutzky neighborhood boomed from 1910 to 1930. Kerry Conley, owner of a growing camera factory, moved into the neighborhood in 1910, as did many people who worked at the factory. The Kutzkys generously gave the city twenty-seven acres along Cascade Creek for a city park. The neighborhood became home to many nurses, medical residents, and other people employed by Mayo Clinic.

Subsequent to the development of Pill Hill and other early neighborhoods in downtown Rochester, IBM's arrival and employment of 1,800 people spurred several developments and new elementary schools with more of a suburban feeling. Elton Hills, Sunset Terrace, Gage, and Country Club neighborhoods and schools were built in the 1960s to accommodate the growth. Elton Hills was developed by Carl and Vivian Elford and Fullerton Lumberyard, combining their names to make Elton Hills. It was the first neighborhood in Rochester, other than Plummer Circle, not to be laid out in a grid. Instead, the streets curve and include many cul-de-sacs. This new design was seen as progressive to those living there and frustrating for many others in town accustomed to a straight street and avenue system.

At the same time that IBM was growing in the early 1960s, Rochester welcomed its first shopping mall, Apache Mall. On October 16, 1969, the Mayo High School Band performed for the more than 20,000 people who attended the grand opening. Boasting of being fully "climate controlled," the new Rochester indoor mall followed a national trend that began with the development of Southdale Shopping Center in Edina, Minnesota, in 1956. The increasing property taxes and the cost and availability of parking motivated retailers to leave downtown.

Rochester's Apache Mall, 1983. *HCOC*

Although the mall was the first shopping center that offered indoor shopping from store to store, Rochester had been a leader in innovative shopping experiences for some time. In 1956, Miracle Mile, an outdoor shopping center, was built two blocks west of Saint Marys Hospital. It was the first shopping center built in Minnesota outside of the Twin Cities. A large Red Owl grocery store was one of the anchor stores. A hardware store, a drugstore, clothing stores, and a five and dime variety store opened at Miracle Mile. Donaldson's Department Store anchored the other end of the mall and installed the city's first escalator. Crossroads, Silver Lake, and Northgate followed, developing outside of the immediate downtown area. In 1963, Sears became the first department store to move from downtown to Crossroads, where they offered ample free parking.

Apache Mall offered indoor, climate-controlled shopping. The mall, a joint development effort between local investors and the Apache Corporation in Minneapolis, opened in late 1969 on forty-six acres, holding 540,000 square feet and forty-five stores, including three large stores that moved from downtown: Montgomery Ward, Woolworth, and JCPenney. They were soon joined by a Red Owl grocery store. There was space for fifty stores at the opening, including a mix of locally owned shops and larger chain stores.

The Apache corporation's name is not affiliated with the Native tribe, but rather it is an appropriation of the tribe's name; it is based on the initials of the founders, three men from Minneapolis: Truman Anderson, Raymond Plank, and Charles Arnao. A secretary in their firm suggested that they add "che" to the initials of their last names, "apa," to form Apache. The corporation had real estate holdings in Minneapolis, including an interest in Foshay Tower. Ultimately, Apache Corporation grew into one of the country's largest oil and gas companies, with headquarters in Houston, Texas. In 1977, the Apache Corporation sold the mall to MEPC American Properties, Inc., a Dallas-based company.

Downtown businesses felt threatened by the mall's opening and the move of retail there. A referendum to fund redevelopment downtown, including a mall downtown, did not pass in 1969. Concerns about the waning vitality of downtown were well founded. Dayton's (later bought by Macy's) moved from its multistory premier department store downtown to become another anchor store at the mall in 1972.

Stores came and went at Apache Mall over the next twenty-five years, but the general direction was growth. By the twenty-fifth anniversary in 1994, 1,600 people were employed at the mall, and another five hundred were hired each Christmas holiday season, catering to the 300,000 people who shopped there. One hundred stores filled 760,000 square feet, and a food court—an innovation—had been added in 1991.

In the late 1980s and well into the 1990s, big box stores—Walmart, Best Buy, Target, Toys "R" Us—began to chip away at the retail market. Apache Mall was bolstered in 1991 when Sears built a 133,000-square-foot anchor store, but in 1998, the mall was sold again to another out-of-state owner, this time to General Growth Properties, one of the largest mall owners in the country. Just over a decade later, in 2009, it went bankrupt. Sears closed in 2014. By this time, Amazon and online shopping, in addition to the big box stores, were cutting into the retail market. Brookfield Properties, headquartered in New York and one of the largest property development and management firms in the world, became the owner of Apache Mall. There is frequent turnover in stores, and the out-of-state ownership has the potential for the mall to feel more like someone else's investment without a commitment to the community. The arrival of Scheels sporting goods store filled the large void left when Sears closed. JCPenney is the only store from the original retailers who opened in the mall and has remained for over fifty years.

In 1993, just as IBM's presence began waning and the market was tightening for the mall, Rochester was named *Money Magazine*'s "Best Place to Live" in the United States, a ranking based on scores for health, crime, economy, housing, education, transit, weather, leisure, and arts. Rochester was in the top ten of the three hundred towns for three of the categories—health, crime, and education—resulting in an overall score that placed the city at the top. Not surprisingly, Rochester's lowest score was for weather. Writers for the *Chicago Tribune* made a trip to Rochester and were surprised at "how ordinary" Rochester was. "Everything you can do here—get a job, have a nice house, breathe clean air, send children to decent schools and jog safely—used to be part of the American Dream. Now that's a premium . . . a trip to Normalville might be worthwhile, to see how much Elsewhere has slipped."

In contrast, a column in the *Rochester Post Bulletin* in response to the award noted that *Money Magazine*'s readers value "low taxes, housing appreciation and strong state government." The columnist complained that Rochester was a "center for wealthy hypochondriacs" and that people leave the city in droves on the weekends in search of entertainment. The columnist also noted Rochester's lack of used bookstores, yoga centers, interesting grocery stores, and coffeehouses.

Rochester remained high in the *Money* rankings as a most livable city for a few years, ranking fifteenth in 2019, but was not on the list in 2020 or 2021, although several other cities in Minnesota appear. The magazine does not disclose enough information to determine which criterion caused Rochester to drop in the rankings.

CHAPTER 8

City of Innovation, Collaboration, and Hope

Mother Alfred Moes's response to the cyclone hitting Rochester in 1883 was radical and transformative. Subsequently, Mayo Clinic and IBM spawned a plethora of innovations in medicine and technology. These are not the only originators in Rochester. From those first millers who rerouted the river, to the Women's Club that installed one of the first public restrooms, to the city's early adoption of public health initiatives such as recycling and pasteurization, Rochester became a place to create and implement new ideas. Often collaborations evolved as opportunities arose.

Conley Camera might be considered the first high-tech company in town outside of Mayo Clinic. Kerry Conley graduated from Chicago Ophthalmic College and Hospital in 1891 and began fitting customers with eyeglasses in his jewelry store in his hometown—Spring Valley, Minnesota, about thirty miles south of Rochester. Around the same time, in 1886, another resident of the Spring Valley area, Richard Sears, started a mail-order catalog business after moving to Minneapolis. Watches and jewelry were the first products he sold. The business evolved into Sears, Roebuck and Company and moved its headquarters to Chicago.

In 1898, Kerry and his brother, Fred Conley, secured a patent for a magazine camera—a box camera that held several glass or metal plates, allowing the photographer to make multiple photo exposures without reloading the camera. They began production in Spring Valley in 1899.

Conley Camera Company's factory, 1904. *HCOC*

A woman working at the Conley factory, 1913. *HCOC*

By 1903, they introduced a camera that held twelve aluminum plates and silent shutters. In the same year, Sears, Roebuck and Company chose Conley Camera Company as its supplier for cameras. In 1904, Conley Camera moved to Rochester to take advantage of better access to rail service and workers. Starting with sixteen employees, the company expanded production in a brick building in downtown Rochester, and by 1907, 135 people were employed, producing 28,000 cameras, 80,000 plate holders, and 1,000 silent shutters.

In 1907, the Conley Camera Company also began collaborating with Dr. Louis B. Wilson, a pathologist hired by the Mayos. Dr. Wilson was interested in using photography to document specimens and surgical procedures. Their first collaboration resulted in a specimen camera for stereoscopic photography. The following year, they began marketing the Queen City Specimen Camera No. 42, which included a posing tank to keep specimens submerged while images were taken. The camera weighed seven hundred pounds.

The Conley Camera Company expanded their product line to include a panoramic camera, telephones, and other electrical apparatuses. The growth required it to move out of downtown Rochester to a new plant on the north edge of town. Shortly afterward, Kerry Conley's health began to fail, and Sears acquired the company. In its next phase, the company continued to collaborate with Dr. Wilson on medical products, and, looking for new technologies and markets, it expanded into the production of phonographs. In 1928, the plant produced 75,000 phonographs. In the 1930s, the company produced the Hemp Body Massager and toy phones. Neither product line was very successful, and production was

The name "Queen City" was first applied to Rochester in the late 1870s, possibly by Delbert Darling, owner of a business school and photography institute, who used it as a sales slogan. The name stuck for a few decades and then almost entirely disappeared until recently, when several contemporary businesses have adopted it. "Med City" is the other common nickname for Rochester.

short-lived. Camera production had also become very competitive when Eastman Kodak Company grew in the market.

In 1940, Sears, Roebuck and Company sold its interest in the Rochester company to Glen Waters, who renamed it Waters Conley Company. They added engineers to the staff and expanded into a new field, affordable home stereo phonographs. The Phabulous Phonola became one of their most popular products.

Sales were boosted during World War II, when the company was granted contracts with the Signal Corp of Army Engineers. Initially, the government contracted for the production of 40,000 emergency fishing tackle containers, truck engine parts, and armored tank interphone systems. In 1943, the company received a subcontract from Western Electric to participate in the design and production of a drone called the Bat, the first fully automated, guided missile used in combat. In 1945, Waters Conley, Inc., was awarded the Army-Navy "E" Award, for excellence in production, given to only five percent of the private companies that had contracts with the army and navy.

In the postwar period, Waters Conley began production of a home pasteurizer; collaborations with Mayo Clinic scientists continued, resulting in the creation of a camera for counting red blood cells, an endoscopic camera, a special camera for photographing eyes, an aseptic camera for use in surgery, and a blood oxygenator. In 1957, production of the phonographs increased to two thousand units a day with four hundred employees. In 1960, a portion of Waters Conley, Inc., was sold to Telex Communications, and the remainder became known as Waters Instruments, Inc. By the 1990s, the headquarters of both companies left Rochester, but Waters Medical Systems LLC, affiliated with a French firm, remains in Rochester with a product line of organ profusion and preservation systems that support organ transplantation.

Innovative companies have continued to spawn in Rochester, often the result of collaborative efforts. Two pharmacists from a Mayo-affiliated hospital started Pharmaceutical Specialties, Inc., in 1974 to produce a skin-care product for people with dermatological conditions and skin sensitivities. In 1980, they began producing Vanicream, a thick moisturizing cream without fragrances, dyes, or preservatives. They marketed it to dermatologists, who recommended it to patients. Forty years later, market demand for this product is increasing to meet the needs of people with allergies and sensitivities who are seeking products with as few additives as possible—in this case, free of dyes, fragrances, lanolin, parabens, formaldehyde releasers, and even gluten. With an adaptive, innovative, and collaborative focus, Pharmaceutical Specialties, Inc., continues to expand through its research labs and distribute twenty-three unique products to medical facilities and major retail distributors worldwide. It is one example of the three hundred small to medium-size manufacturing and distribution companies in the area that make up a rich network in the shadow of Mayo Clinic.

Mayo Clinic's growth from the original partnership between Mother Alfred Moes and Dr. William Worrall Mayo and his sons has endured. In the 1980s, Mayo began a new growth strategy. It legally merged with the hospitals, including Saint Marys, to improve efficiencies and provider reimbursement, and it opened clinics in Arizona and Florida. It also continued regional growth throughout southeastern Minnesota, northern Iowa, and western Wisconsin. Mayo Clinic's laboratories began accepting specimens from other medical facilities in the 1970s, leading the way for an international presence that now includes clinical facilities in London and Abu Dhabi. Along with decades of growth, Mayo Clinic Rochester has not lost its reputation for the highest quality of care; it has been ranked the No. 1 "best hospital" in the country by *U.S. News & World Report* since 2016. Throughout its system, Mayo annually treats 1.3 million patients from every state and 130 countries, counting 4,700 physicians and scientists within its staff of 73,000 employees.

Mayo demonstrates its commitment to education and research through its medical school, physician residencies, and fellowships that train future doctors. It has programs—some in collaboration with other institutions of higher education—to train nurses, physical therapists, pharmacists, laboratory and imaging technicians, phlebotomists, and others providing patient care. Mayo's research programs represent another shield of its three-part logo. Its list of the clinic's 150 top contributions to medicine, created at the time of its 150th anniversary in 2014, includes frozen sections in laboratory medicine that improve outcomes in surgery, cortisone (for which the physicians won a Nobel Prize in medicine), the G suit developed during World War II, heart bypass surgery, hip replacements, CT scanning, and a DNA test for anthrax. Most recently, Mayo Clinic was a leader in developing diagnostic testing for COVID-19.

In addition to local initiatives, Minnesota state government was engaged to support development in Rochester. Destination Medical Center (DMC), a twenty-year economic development project created to turbocharge business growth, was approved in 2013. The collaboration between Mayo Clinic, the State of Minnesota, Olmsted County, and the City of Rochester intends to strategically invest over $50 billion in infrastructure to attract private investment, create 30,000 jobs, and secure Rochester's position as an internationally recognized destination for health and wellness for patients, visitors, and the community. The government funding portion primarily supports infrastructure: roads, sewers, water.

By 2019, DMC funding contributed to opening One Discovery Square, an innovative office building not far from Mayo Clinic where start-ups, Mayo partners, companies new to Rochester, and University of Minnesota Rochester students and faculty can meet and learn from each other. Companies considering coming to Rochester look for assurance that there will be an available workforce. A nonprofit, Collider, emerged to assist entrepreneurs with space and support. They leased the second floor of the brick building once occupied by the Conley Camera factory, reigniting a spirit of innovation in that space. Larger corporations with international footprints, such as Google and Philips, have also opened offices in Rochester to engage in multifaceted collaborations.

Not everyone in Rochester appreciates the DMC. Some business owners feel that it places too much emphasis on bringing in outside companies, rather than providing funding to existing Rochester businesses that have the potential to grow. Some are concerned about the city's capacity to sustain the improvements once the funding has been spent. Others argue that new construction should be put on hold until the full impact of the COVID-19 pandemic is known; in 2021, Mayo Clinic began permanently reassigning thousands of downtown employees to remote work, emptying many office buildings at the same time new space is being built.

Given this controversy, Mayor Kim Norton, who advocated for DMC when she was a state representative, sounded a lot like Mother Alfred when she was recently interviewed: "We need to take advantage of this moment. The COVID pandemic has everything laid bare; we have the opportunity to make [Rochester] what we want it to be." Aware of deep political divides and growing economic disparities, she advocates for continuing to be innovative and partnering on solutions: "We need to work on acknowledging and righting the wrongs of the past and present, not erase the past." Mayor Norton points to the shortage of affordable housing and recent efforts to address the needs of people affected by homelessness. She noted that hundreds of people came to town hall meetings advocating for improved housing conditions, and she sees the solutions developing in continued partnerships among government, private businesses, churches, and nonprofit organizations. Noting the high expectations that Rochester needs to meet, the mayor emphasized, "People come here for hope," and we don't want to let them down.

Somewhat surprisingly, Rochester's skyline includes a recently renovated ninety-year-old water tower painted to resemble an ear of corn. The bright yellow 149-foot-tall structure, which holds 50,000 gallons, stands on the south edge of downtown, next to the county fairgrounds. It was built in 1931 by a vegetable canning company and used by its successors, important to the area's agriculture business for almost ninety years. When the plant closed in 2018, the county purchased the property, demolished the buildings, and (after considerable debate) spent $400,000 to refurbish the water tower. Residents had differing opinions about the landmark.

The corncob water tower and the Rochester skyline, 2021. *Photo by Andrew Link,* Rochester Post Bulletin, *June 2018*

Some people felt the corncob tower was tacky and should come down; others felt that it remains an important tribute to the agricultural origins of Rochester—although wheat was the primary crop when mills operated along the Zumbro River banks and sparked the city's growth.

Rochester's skyline reveals a lot of the story of the city: the corncob water tower, Saint Marys Hospital, the iconic Plummer Building that stands in contrast and connection to the newer shiny Mayo Clinic Gonda Building, Assisi Heights convent, the blue IBM campus that is emptying, and many hotels and restaurants providing hospitality to more than a million visitors every year, some of them in wheelchairs, others on their phones calling home with updates while they navigate the skyways between appointments. The Zumbro River winds through town, past the quiet woods of Indian Heights, while V-shaped flocks of Canada geese fly overhead. Less visible are the Dakota people, Potter's Field, the day center for people affected by homelessness, and the disparities in housing, health care, education, and income that do not appear in the form of a building or road.

Visually apparent in the juxtaposition of the corncob water tower and shiny medical center buildings is the opportunity to lean on the traditions of innovation, collaboration, and hope as Rochester forges a future in the context of a global pandemic, rising political divisiveness, and heightened awareness of racial injustice. The potential to actualize the highest ideals of those who came before and those living and working in Rochester today is real.

For Further Reading

Readers interested in knowing more about Rochester history will find much of interest in the sources specific to each chapter that are listed below. These notes also provide sources for quotations.

Abbreviations:

HCOC—History Center of Olmsted County
MNHS—Minnesota Historical Society
RPB—Rochester Post Bulletin

Knowing a Place, Knowing Ourselves

Quotation: p. 2, "depredations of the Indians": *Rochester Republican,* August 27, 1862.

1. Indian Heights

Gary Clayton Anderson, *Minnesota Massacre: The Dakota War of 1862, the Most Violent Ethnic Conflict in American History* (Norman: University of Oklahoma Press, 2019); Gary Clayton Anderson and Alan R. Woolworth, eds., *Through Dakota Eyes: Narrative Accounts of the Minnesota Indian War of 1862* (St. Paul: MNHS Press, 1988); Lavina Eastlick, *Thrilling Incidents of the Indian War of 1862: Being a Personal Narrative of the Outrages and Horrors Witnessed by Mrs. L. Eastlick in Minnesota* (Minneapolis: Atlas Steam Press, 1864); Friends of Indian Heights, "Park History," www.foih.org/history; Bertha L. Heilbron, "Documentary Panorama,"

Minnesota History 30, no. 1 (March 1949): 14–23; Indian Heights Park Master Plan, City of Rochester, March 2017; John R. Isch, *You Had to Have Been There and Lived It: Panoramas of the 1862 US–Dakota War* (New Ulm, MN: John R. Isch, 2019); Joseph A. Leonard, *History of Olmsted County, Minnesota: Together with Sketches of Many of Its Pioneers, Citizens, Families and Institutions* (Chicago: Goodspeed Historical Association, 1910); Mrs. William Brown Melony, "Mrs. Mayo, Wilderness Mother," *The Delineator* 85 (September 1914): 46; John Stevens, "Stevens' Great Tableau Paintings Representing the Indian Massacre in Minnesota in 1862," scripts on file at HCOC; Gwen Westerman and Bruce White, *Mni Sota Makoce: The Land of the Dakota* (St. Paul: MNHS Press, 2012).

Quotations: p. 10, "For one or two years": Leonard, *History*, 637; p. 10, "a bluff nearly west": Leonard, *History*, 638; p. 11, "unfeeling savages," "the Indians all left," and "small parties": Leonard, *History*, 639; p. 11, 12, "going to Minnesota" and "the room": Marion L. Sloan, "Reminiscences of Miss Marion L. Sloan," interview by Mrs. Julia Ratcliff, February 24, 1937, on file at HCOC; p. 12, "most of the red men": Leonard, *History*, 637; p. 14, "teams along the road" through "the difficulty": Leonard, *History*, 637; p. 14, "The Sioux Indians": *Annual Message of Governor Ramsey to the Legislature of Minnesota, Delivered January 9th, 1863* (St. Paul: William R. Marshall, 1862), 12; p. 14, "The Indian is": *Rochester Republican*, September 10, 1862; p. 15, "What Shall Be Done": *Rochester Record*, October 15, 1862; p. 15, "The people of this State": *Rochester Record*, November 12, 1862; p. 15, "serious attack was made": *Rochester Record*, November 19, 1862; p. 16, "general good conduct" and "following, overtaking": *Rochester Post*, August 6, 1863; p. 18, "Who dressed your wounds?": Melony, "Mrs. Mayo," 9; p. 18, "seven Indians": Melony, "Mrs. Mayo," 9, 46; p. 23, "life-size pictures": Leonard, *History*, 192; p. 24, "to give the necessary": *Rochester Daily Bulletin*, October 7, 1921; p. 24, "Murder of Mr. Cook": *RPB*, November 8, 1927; p. 24, "Thrilling Incidents": *RPB*, November 28, 1927; p. 25, "The odds": *RPB*, June 3, 1949; p. 25, "Massacre Scene," to "I saw it": *RPB*, May 5, 1950; p. 25, "How the West": *Life*, May 4, 1959; p. 26, "shallow and covered": Sloan, "Reminiscences."

2. Waterways, Roadways, and Railways to Development

Helen B. Clapesattle, *The Doctors Mayo* (Minneapolis: University Minnesota Press, 1941); Arthur J. Larsen, "Roads and Trails in the Minnesota Triangle, 1849–60," *Minnesota History* 11 (December 1930): 387–411; Jim Scribbins, *The 400 Story: Chicago & North Western's Premier Passenger Trains* (Glendale, CA: PTJ Books of Interurban Press, 1982); files on stagecoaches, mills, railroads, Silver Lake, George and Henrietta Head, Zumbro River floods, and others, HCOC.

Quotations: p. 30, "Towns sprang": Larsen, "Roads and Trails," 396; p. 30, "inhabited by": Larsen, "Roads and Trails," 390; p. 32, Rochester's naming: Tom Weber, "Nathaniel Rochester's History in New York Becomes More Clear," *RPB*, January 25, 2022; p. 33, "aghast" through "found their way": Amelia Ullmann, "Frontier Business Trip: Reminiscences of Mrs. Joseph Ullmann," *Minnesota History* 34 (Spring 1954): 18; p. 34, "Rochester is": *St. Paul Advertiser*, March 14, 1857; p. 41, "check hemorrhage": Clapesattle, *Doctors Mayo*, 349; p. 41, In 1892, a train: these stories are recounted in Clapesattle, *Doctors Mayo*, 350; p. 42, "Dr. Mayo's train": Clapesattle, *Doctors Mayo*, 489–90; p. 42, "travel perfection" and "possessing the resilient": Chicago & North Western Railroad, "Rochester 400" advertising brochure, 1930, HCOC; p. 45, "there is only so much room": Minutes of the Rochester and Olmsted County Public Safety Council, March 20, 1946, HCOC.

3. Out of Destruction

Ken Allsen, *A Century of Elegance: Ellerbe Residential Design in Rochester, Minnesota* (Minneapolis: Ellerbe Becket, 2009); Ken Allsen, *Master Architect: The Life and Works of Harold Crawford* (Rochester: History Center of Olmsted County, 2014); Ken Allsen, *Old College Street: The Historic Heart of Rochester, Minnesota* (Charleston, SC: History Press, 2012); Clapesattle, *The Doctors Mayo;* Thomas F. Ellerbe, *The Ellerbe Tradition: Seventy Years of Architecture & Engineering* (Minneapolis: Ellerbe, Inc., 1980); Jeffrey E. Nelson and Steve F. Wilstead, "Alice Magaw (Kessle): Her Life In and Out of the Operating Room," *American Association of*

Nurse Anesthetists Journal 77 (February 2009): 12–16; Clark J. Pahlas, *The Unique Voice of Service: The Story of the Kahler Corporation, Rochester, Minnesota* (Rochester: Custom Print, 1964); Ingrid Peterson, OSF, *Keeping the Memory Green: Mother Alfred Moes and the Sisters of Saint Francis, Rochester, Minnesota* (Rochester: Sisters of Saint Francis, 2013); "Rochester's Disaster," *Rochester Post*, August 27, 1883; Marietta Sonnenberg, "Motherhouse of Sisters of St. Francis Nears Completion," *RPB*, March 23, 1955; [Philip K. Strand], *A Century of Caring: Saint Marys Hospital of Rochester, Minnesota, 1889–1989* (Rochester: Saint Marys Hospital, 1989); Ellen Whelan, OSF, *The Sisters' Story: Saint Marys Hospital–Mayo Clinic, 1889 to 1939* (Rochester: Mayo Foundation for Medical Education and Research, 2002); Virginia M. Wright-Peterson, *Women of Mayo Clinic: The Founding Generation* (St. Paul: MNHS Press, 2016).

Quotations: p. 52, "No dirge": *Rochester Post*, August 27, 1883; p. 56, "white neighbor" and "It was a rough": Melony, "Mrs. Mayo," 9; p. 60, "everything about": *Rochester Post*, October 4, 1889; p. 60, "The cause": Whelan, *Sisters' Story*, 67; p. 61, "Ardent Protestants": Whelan, *Sisters' Story*, 68; p. 61, "a woman of rare courage": Nora H. Guthrey, *Medicine and Its Practitioners in Olmsted County Prior to 1900* (Rochester: n.p., 1951), 117; p. 62, "too young" and "was not a man": Judith Hartzell, *Mrs. Charlie: The Other Mayo* (Rochester: Mayo Clinic, 2019), 15; p. 64, "Her work drew": Clapesattle, *Doctors Mayo*, 427; p. 64, "mother of anesthesia": Virginia S. Thatcher, *History of Anesthesia with Emphasis on the Nurse Specialist* (Philadelphia: Lippincott, 1957), 57; p. 66, "The best interest": quoted in Clapesattle, *Doctors Mayo*, 531; p. 68, "are conducive to": *Rochester Post & Record*, March 7, 1914; p. 68, "which will produce": *Rochester Daily Bulletin*, March 7, 1914; p. 68, A medical journal article: Richard Olding Beard, "The Mayo Clinic Building at Rochester," *Journal-Lancet* 34 (1914); p. 77, "is a tremendous": *RPB*, March 23, 1955.

4. Potter's Field

Carl Adams, "Lincoln's First Freed Slave: A Review of *Bailey v. Cromwell*, 1841," *Journal of the Illinois State Historical Society* 101, no. 3–4

(2008): 235–59; "Anent Marie Dalberg," *Rochester Post & Record*, December 18, 1903; Governor's Interracial Commission of Minnesota, *The Negro and His Home in Minnesota* (St. Paul: The Commission, 1947), https://www.leg.mn.gov/docs/pre2003/other/i540.pdf; History of Oakwood Cemetery, unpublished pamphlet at HCOC; Oakwood Cemetery, ledger; Olmsted County court, sheriff's, and death records for Dalberg case; Rochester State Hospital file and pamphlets, HCOC.

Quotations: p. 79, "a colored man": *Rochester Record and Union*, May 17, 1898; p. 80, "books and reading matter": Leonard, *History*, 220; p. 83, "out of shame": *Rochester Post & Record*, March 27, 1903; p. 83, "happy, light hearted girl": *Rochester Post & Record*, December 18, 1903.

5. More Hidden Stories

Jake Blumgart, "Redlining Didn't Happen Quite the Way We Thought it Did," *Governing: The Future of States and Localities*, September 21, 2021; *The Crucible* (Rochester High School student paper), November 19, 1918; Rick Dahl, "Legacy of the Avalon Hotel," *RPB*, January 22, 2011; Juliet Eisendrath Papers, Social Work Collection, Mayo Clinic Historical Unit (contains reference to the deposit Mayo required of Black, Jewish, and Greek people); Elizabeth Dorsey Hatle, *The Ku Klux Klan in Minnesota* (Charleston, SC: History Press, 2013); Ku Klux Klan folder, HCOC; Virginia Gibson Mendenhall, interview, Rochester, MN, January 2020; Thelma M. Robinson, *Nisei Cadet Nurse of World War II: Patriotism in Spite of Prejudice* (Boulder, CO: Black Swan Mill Press, 2005); *Rochester Daily Bulletin*, October 3, 1918; George Thompson, interview, Rochester, MN, December 22, 2019; Tom Weber, "1963: Civil Rights Tumult: Rochester March Marred by Eggs, Burning Cross," *RPB*, January 13, 2018; Sister Ellen Whelan, OSF, *The Sisters' Story, Part 2: Saint Marys Hospital–Mayo Clinic, 1939 to 1980* (Rochester: Mayo Foundation for Medical Education and Research, 2007).

Quotations: p. 89–90, "The Everlasting," "as good as," "enter an omnibus," and "wrong, if not": *Rochester City Post*, January 6, 1866; p. 92, "No Negros allowed": *RPB*, March 11, 2016; p. 94, "You're headed": *RPB*, August 23, 1963; p. 94, "LET'S HAVE NO MORE": *RPB*, August 24,

1963; p. 94, "Rochester is known": Catherine Atkinson, Letter to the Editor, *RPB*, August 26, 1963; p. 97, "The reputation": Governor's Interracial Commission of Minnesota, *The Negro and His Home in Minnesota*, 12; p. 98, "None of said": Randy Petersen, "Mapping History," *RPB*, March 31, 2021; p. 100, "1st Negro": *RPB*, undated clipping on file at HCOC; p. 102, "I know your address" and "something more": *RPB*, October 5, 2020; p. 104, "outstanding" and "the hospital": Whelan, *Sisters' Story, Part 2*, 56; p. 104, "Time to Revise": *RPB*, November 3, 1986; p. 105, article about a lesbian couple: *RPB*, July 12, 1997.

6. Women Take the Lead

Florence Barker, "The Women's League of Rochester, Minnesota: History and Development," unpublished manuscript, HCOC; Clapesattle, *Doctors Mayo*; William D. Green, *The Children of Lincoln: White Paternalism and the Limits of Black Opportunity in Minnesota, 1860–1876* (Minneapolis: University of Minnesota Press, 2018); Guthrey, *Medicine and Its Practitioners*; Anne Halliwell, "50 Years of Beer at Schuster Brewing Company," *RPB*, March 9, 2018; League of Women Voters, *Taking the Lead: Rochester Women in Public Policy, 1970–1990* (St. Cloud, MN: Polaris Publishing, 2012); Janice McFarland, "Women Played Major but Unsung Roles in Rochester," *RPB*, August 5, 1983; "Rochester Reaches $1 Million Settlement with Former Police Lieutenant," Med City Beat, September 19, 2017; "Woman Suffrage," *Rochester Post*, November 2 and December 28, 1877; Wright-Peterson, *Women of Mayo Clinic*.

The Women's History Circle of the History Center of Olmsted County, a group dedicated to collecting, preserving, and sharing the contributions of women, held several forums in 2019 and 2020, including one that invited current and previously elected officials to speak. The recording is on file at the History Center. Amy Caucutt gathered much of the information for the 2019–20 Women's Suffrage exhibit at History Center of Olmsted County (which includes the "Mrs. Witherstine" quote on p. 111) and for the book *Taking the Lead*.

Quotations: p. 107, "a thoroughly competent," "the highest opinion," and "female delicacy": *Northwest Journal of Medicine and Surgery* 1

(1870–81): 52–53; p. 108, "was lowery" and "intelligent mothers": quoted in *Rochester Post*, December 28, 1877; p. 109, "There is no reason": *Rochester Post*, November 2, 1877; p. 111, "Mrs. Witherstine": *Olmsted County Democrat*, [n.d.], 1911; p. 111, "inconceivable": *RPB*, February 28, 1974; p. 111, "women have as good": essay at W. Bruce Fye Center for the History of Medicine, Mayo Clinic; p. 114, "great strength": Halliwell, "50 Years of Beer"; p. 115, "is not a believer": *Rochester Daily Post and Record*, April 10, 1913; p. 123, "We are finally": *RPB*, December 31, 1991; p. 123–24, "When the expression": Med City Beat, September 19, 2017.

7. Big Blue Comes to Town

106 Group, "Rochester Historical Contexts," report submitted to the City of Rochester, 2014; IBM Rochester News, General Systems Division, January 1976, HCOC; Jeff Kiger, "Apache Mall Introduced Modern Retail to Rochester Fifty Years Ago," *RPB*, October 10, 2019; Arthur L. Norberg and Jeffrey R. Yost, *IBM Rochester: Half a Century of Innovation* (Rochester: IBM, 2006).

Quotations: p. 125, "erect a huge plant," "the high degree," and "delighted": *RPB*, February 8, 1956; p. 128–29, "IBM Dispels" through "is said to have encountered": *RPB*, September 12, 1963; p. 134, "climate controlled": *RPB*, September 17, 1968 and October 10, 2019; p. 136, "how ordinary": *Chicago Tribune*, September 19, 1993; p. 137, "low taxes" and "center for": quoted in *Chicago Tribune*, September 19, 1993.

8. City of Innovation, Collaboration, and Hope

"Contributions to Medicine," available in the Toolkit at Mayo Clinic History & Heritage, history.mayoclinic.org; Destination Medical Center (DMC) website, dmc.mn; Jeff Kiger, "Vanicream Continues Its Quiet Med City Growth," *RPB*, March 19, 2021; Janet Moore, "Rochester's Destination Medical Center Forges Ahead, Despite COVID-19," *Minneapolis Star Tribune*, February 8, 2021; Matthew Stolle, "The Ear-of-Corn Tower: Why Does Rochester Care So Much About It?," *RPB*, July 20, 2021.

Quotations: p. 145, "We need to take advantage" through "People come here": Mayor Kim Norton, interview, October 15, 2021.

Acknowledgments

One of my earliest memories is of my mother, Marlys Peterson, taking me to the public library. As I gazed up at the building—with its Gothic trimmings and a stone owl peering down from its perch on the roof above the entrance—I thought it was a castle filled with books. My life is much richer for having been introduced to the magic and power of stories at a young age. I am deeply grateful to my mother and all of the librarians and archivists who keep our stories, especially Krista Lewis at the History Center of Olmsted County, Renee Ziemer at the W. Bruce Fye Center for the History of Medicine at Mayo Clinic, Susan Hansen at Rochester Public Library, and Sister Lauren Weinandt, OSF, Sisters of Saint Francis of Rochester, Minnesota, who at one hundred years old is the longest-serving employee at Saint Marys Hospital, Mayo Clinic Campus.

A cadre of passionate volunteers at the History Center of Olmsted County and writers and historians in the area are dedicated to keeping Rochester's past alive, and several of them contributed to my research. I am most grateful to Sean Kettlekamp, Lee Hilgendorf, George B. Thompson, Tom Weber, Ken Allsen, Amy Caucutt, Laura Deering, Joyce Gibbs, Robert Haeussinger, Amy Jo Hahn, Virginia Mendenhall, Leo Noser, Christine Rule, Dr. Paul Scanlon, Tim Schmitt, Romayne Thompson, Linda Willihnganz, and members of the Rochester IBM Alumni Club, who have gleaned and shared stories and information valuable to me in assembling this version of Rochester's history.

I am deeply grateful to Minnesota Historical Society Press Editor in Chief Ann Regan for her extensive knowledge, sharp pen, and constant encouragement. This book is better in many ways because of her touch. Among other challenges, Ann had to endure my desire to tell history out of chronological order, my penchant for using antiquated terms for historical impact, and my tendency to write too many passive sentences. She put up with a lot. I am also appreciative of all of the contributions by the press's staff and freelancers who copyedit, design covers and pages, index, promote, and do a myriad of other things from the time an author sends them several thousand words to the day the book magically appears.

This book would not have been possible without many good friends and family. Gretchen McCoy dug through the archives with me and read multiple drafts. Dawn Littleton provided tremendous input during some of the most challenging aspects of my research. Carole Stiles, Yuko Taniguchi, and Pamela Presley encouraged me along the way. Gifted photographer and friend Brendan Bush captured and restored images. Chancellor Lori Carrell and the students, staff, and faculty at University of Minnesota Rochester continue to inspire me. My longtime friend Marsha Hall has been around for some of the best and worst stories of my life. My siblings are terrific: Ann Garritty, Sandy Kelm, and Roger Peterson.

The Sisters of Saint Francis in Rochester, Minnesota, remain an inspirational beacon for Rochester and for me. Sister Linda Wieser has been of special support, especially in light of the loss of my dear mentor Sister Ingrid Peterson, who remains an illuminating guide. Memories of my husband, Ralph Wright-Peterson, and my father, John V. Peterson, are with me, as well, especially when I walk at Oakwood Cemetery.

My new canine friend, Flash Griffin, gives me looks of true boredom while I tap away on the keyboard for more hours a day than sometimes seems humanly possible.

My daughter, Kristina, who is one of the nurses working in public health during this pandemic, continues to inspire me with her resilience, dedication, and compassion. Harper and Heath are two of the most fantastic grandchildren a grandmother could have. They inspire me with their boundless energy, curiosity, and hope. Some of the best advice I have been given during the pandemic and while writing this book came from Harper: "Be the positive energy when you can."

Index

Italicized page numbers indicate an image or its caption.